MISUNDERESTIMATED & OVERUNDERAPPRECIATED

SLOGAN·ANOTHER SLOGAN·SLOGAN·NEW SLOGAN·SLOGAN

SLOGAN·SLOGAN·SLOGAN·SLOGAN·SLOGAN

SLOGAN·SLOGAN·SLOGAN·ANOTHER NEW SLOGAN·SLOGAN

SLOGAN·SLOGAN·SLOGAN·SLOGAN

SLOGAN·SLOGAN·SLOGAN

REVISED SLOGAN·SLOGAN

IRAQ EXIT STRATEGY

MISUNDERESTIMATED & OVERUNDERAPPRECIATED

The George W. Bush Administration as Seen Through the Eyes of the Tribune's Syndicated Editorial Cartoonists

with **Mark Crispin Miller**

Foreword by **Garrison Keillor**
Preface by **Patrick Fitzmaurice**

METRO BOOKS
NEW YORK

Dedication

To cartoonist Doug Marlette, who died in an automobile accident just as this book was going to press. Marlette's great sense of humor and pointed approach to editorial cartooning (which he attributed to "rebellious genes" inherited from "a grandmother bayoneted by a guardsman during a mill strike in the Carolinas") are well represented in these pages and, like the man himself, will be sorely missed.

Publisher's Acknowledgments

Any book of this scope, which covers in words and cartoons two of the most controversial presidential terms in American history, is a massively complicated undertaking and requires the participation of a host of talented and enthusiastic people. If the following list of men and women who made this book possible is incomplete, it is due to oversight rather than design.

A gigantic "thank you!" goes out to the men and women at Tribune Media Services, which represents the work of the editorial cartoonists included here, without whom this project never would have come to be: Mary Elson, Mike Fioritto, Patrick Fitzmaurice, Carol Gardner-Lopez, Alice Singleton, Steve Tippie, and John Twohey.

Likewise, heartfelt thanks go to Leila Rahimi, from Garrison Keillor's team, whose patience and persistence were instrumental in putting the final touches to this book.

Last but not least, three full-throated cheers to all the editorial cartoonists hard at work exposing the scandalous, venal, underhanded, pea-brained, ill-intentioned, embarrassing, and frequently hilarious—at least, when seen in a certain light—shenanigans of our public officials, whether elected or…otherwise. Without the tireless efforts of these artists, the light of day might never shine on some of officialdom's most private places.

ISBN-13: 978-1-4351-0017-6
ISBN-10: 1-4351-0017-4

Designed by Laura Lindgren

Cover design by Jo Obarowski

Printed and bound in China

10 9 8 7 6 5 4 3 2 1

A Cartoon History

Patrick Fitzmaurice
Assistant Editor, Tribune Media Services

Ever since George W. Bush took office, editorial cartoonists have been using the power of the pen to skewer his presidency, one panel at a time. The president has been a rich source of material for these observers of the political scene. To use baseball lingo, the Bush administration has been a fat pitch, and the cartoonists have been swinging away for two terms, producing a batting average that would make Wade Boggs and Tony Gwynn envious.

The visual element can be a powerful weapon for those laying siege to embattled officeholders. The eye is drawn first to pictures, then to words. A political pundit writing a column for the op-ed pages must keep a reader hooked paragraph after paragraph. An editorial cartoonist has no such obligation; his work need only catch a reader's eye for an instant.

In the early 1870s, when groundbreaking editorial cartoonist Thomas Nast was waging a cartoon campaign against corrupt New York politician William M. "Boss" Tweed in the pages of *Harper's Weekly*, Tweed became infuriated by the attacks. "Stop them damned pictures!" Tweed supposedly bellowed to his minions. "I don't care so much what the papers say about me. My constituents can't read. But, damn it, they can see pictures!"

Contemporary political cartoons appeal to a more literate group of readers than Boss Tweed's constituents. But still, we love our pictures.

Editorial cartoons are more than just pictures, of course. Almost all of them include words, but the best of the lot use only a handful, to great effect. Some of the most memorable cartoons can deftly critique a politician or a policy in fewer words than you'll find on a single page of a Dr. Seuss book. It's a classic case of less equaling more.

If a single editorial cartoon can convey a large amount of information, then hundreds of editorial cartoons can provide a remarkably thorough narrative. That's the point of the book you're holding in your hands. It tells the story of the Bush presidency through the eyes of some of America's most accomplished editorial cartoonists.

Tribune Media Services, one of the country's largest newspaper syndicates, is fortunate to have an outstanding stable of them, including seven winners of the Pulitzer Prize for editorial cartooning: Paul Conrad, Matt Davies, Walt Handelsman, David Horsey, Dick Locher, Doug Marlette, and Don Wright. Also lending their fine work to this volume are Harry Bliss,

Paul Combs, Taylor Jones, Chan Lowe, Jack Ohman, Drew Sheneman, Wayne Stayskal, Dana Summers, and Dan Wasserman. We've combed through thousands of their drawings and selected several hundred that combine to paint a detailed picture of the Bush presidency. These witty artists have spent the better part of the last decade putting George W. Bush under the microscope, highlighting every flaw in what figures to go down as one of the most flawed presidencies in American history.

There are other characters in this story, of course. Dick Cheney. Karl Rove. Donald Rumsfeld. Condoleezza Rice. John Bolton. Tony Blair. Jacques Chirac. But the star of the show is Dubya, the walking malapropism from deep in the heart of Texas.

Bolstering this collection of cartoons are the observations of two gifted writers, Garrison Keillor and Mark Crispin Miller.

Keillor is the long-time host of the public radio show *A Prairie Home Companion*, which spawned a 2006 movie of the same name. He is also the author of *Lake Wobegon Days* and numerous other books, and he writes a syndicated column for Tribune Media Services in which he frequently criticizes Bush, invariably referring to him as "The Current Occupant." Funny, insightful, self-deprecating, free of flowery language and pretentiousness, Keillor's prose is an American treasure. It's tempting to call his style "plainspoken," but I'm not sure that word does justice to the care and craftsmanship that go into his writing. Keillor will stroll from Point A to a seemingly unrelated Point B,

stopping at far-flung Points C and D along the way, but in the end everything comes together, and you marvel at how he is able to pull it off. (My two-year-old daughter Callyn is similarly smitten with Keillor's work; her favorite book is a children's volume he co-authored, *Daddy's Girl*.)

Miller is a professor of media studies at New York University and the author of several books on public affairs, including 2005's *Fooled Again: How the Right Stole the 2004 Election & Why They'll Steal the Next One Too (Unless We Stop Them)*. A widely published media critic, Miller has also been one of Bush's harshest critics. He deliciously highlighted many of Bush's personal shortcomings—most notably, Dubya's hamhanded use of the English language—in the 2001 book *The Bush Dyslexicon: Observations on a National Disorder*. Miller brings the same sort of acute eye and ear to this book, providing a year-by-year overview of the Bush presidency and wielding words the way a chef in a Japanese steakhouse handles stainless-steel cutlery.

Keillor and Miller are fine emcees, but the cartoonists are the featured performers at this roast, with George W. Bush as the unwitting guest of honor. There's some wonderfully funny material in this book, and as the Bush presidency draws to a close, this cartoon collection is a unique way to review the Bush era and all the gaffes and missteps that marked it.

Thanks for 'tooning in.

Can't Fight This Feeling Anymore

Garrison Keillor

He started out his cartoon life as an idiot, a small petulant man with tiny eyes and big Dumbo ears, a shrimp in a thirty-gallon hat. The first and prevailing comic take on the Current Occupant, Dubya, No. 43, the Shrub, the Decider, was that of Amiable Dunce, Alfred E. ("What? Me Worry?") Neuman in a ten-gallon hat, which was fed by the man's verbal snafus ("the illiteracy level of our children are appalling"), which certainly "resignated" with a lot of people, Republicans as well as Democrats. A small shallow person tries to say important things and gets tangled up in the shrouds of the English language: it's not without its endearing qualities. A man who says, "Life is important and people are important. Both are important." How can you not just sit back and resignate with that?

So you got the cartoon of Cheney teaching the sullen Boy Bush to drive a car. You got the midget Bush next to the towering Colin Powell. In the history of presidential caricature, infantilism is not so unusual, though in the case of FDR or Truman or Ike or JFK, it would have been considered extreme. An infant Ike in the arms of his Vice-President? I don't think so. The Child

Bush, however, was mainstream from the beginning. Here was a man who said, "Too many good docs are getting out of the business. Too many OB-GYNs aren't able to practice their love with women all across this country." (What part of the brain does this emanate from?)

"Anybody who is in a position to serve this country ought to understand the consequences of words," he said, and the consequence of his words was a brisk sale of books of Bushisms. By every bookstore cash register, you found two or three of them, new editions coming out every year. Here was a man of such dim sensibility that he could joke, on a visit to the Amputee Care Center of Brooke Army Medical Center in San Antonio on New Year's Day, 2006, that he himself had suffered an injury "in combat with a cedar. I eventually won. The cedar gave me a little scratch."

The man scraped bottom when Hurricane Katrina wiped out New Orleans while he was on vacation at the ranch and his staff had to put together a video of disaster highlights to get him off the couch and into *Air Force One*. His career had been based on creating low expectations and then meeting them. He was the slacker child who flubbed his way through college and flopped in business and was propped up by family and friends. But Katrina was a blast of reality. The famous headline said, "Bush: One Of The Worst Disasters To Hit The U.S." and many people took that literally. New Orleaneans huddled together in the Superdome were seen on national TV, people stretched out asleep between the goal lines, and a 911 operator broke into sobs describing what it was like to talk to little kids in flooded houses. Two weeks later the President promised to send aid. He also said, "Brownie, you're doing a heck of a job"—which became common slang almost immediately, meaning: "You've messed up about as much as humanly possible." Another Bushism!

With the disaster in Iraq and then Katrina, one of the basic assumptions of American culture fell apart: the competence of Republicans. You might not have always liked Republicans, but you could count on them to manage the bank. They might be lousy tippers, act snooty, talk through their noses, wear spats, and splash mud on you as they raced their Pierce Arrows through the village, but you knew they could do the math. To see them produce a ninny and then follow him loyally into the swamp for eight years was disconcerting.

The problem for cartoonists was that Bush was self-satirizing. Think of the genius cartoonist Walt Kelly and his Pogo who said, "We have met the enemy and he is us." And then along came Bush who said, "Our enemies are innovative and resourceful, and so are we. They never stop thinking about new ways to harm our country and our people, and neither do we." He combined cockiness and poor language skills and the result was a thousand Freudian slips, one after another: "I am surprised, frankly, at the amount of distrust that exists in this town. And I'm sorry it's the case, and I'll work hard to try to elevate it." The man kept telling the truth, except it seemed like a slip of the tongue: "You know, one of the hardest parts of my job is to connect Iraq to the war on terror." Two years into the war, he said, "I think we are welcomed. But it was not a peaceful welcome."

The A.P. ran a story with the hilarious headline: "BUSH URGES CONFIDENCE IN HIS LEADER-SHIP." This is a joke. It's like: "FOX NEWS URGES TRUST IN ITS REPORTING" or "WACO DECLARES AUGUST 'WELCOME TOURISTS' MONTH," and how can mere satirists improve on it? As a leader, he was not in the top fifty percentile, and if his name had been J. Ralph Cooter he'd have been hard put to find work in any of the leadership professions, but there he is, more or less in charge of the shop, or on a first-name basis with those who are, and so long as he refrains from public adultery or wearing a dress to the Easter Egg Roll, he will probably avoid impeachment.

It took time for cartoonists to figure out what to do with the man. To portray him as an idiot or a child was clumsy at best and nothing that any cartoonist would stick with for long, but where to go from there? Occasionally the face became primate-like. And then they hit on the brilliant idea of bushy eyebrows, which made him grown-up and gave him the potential for evil-doing, which is what makes him interesting. Mr. Big Eyebrows stands over a flag-draped coffin and says: "keep up the good work." He is tempted by the video game *Iraq Attack*. The big eyebrows give him a primal edge that comes closer to the real man. Here is the most secretive President since Wilson, who is leery of the free flow of information and of secular institutions, who values tribal loyalty above all and religious tests for public policy, and is more like the ayatollahs and imams than he is like most Americans. Somehow bushy eyebrows take us into that realm, which the childlike moron tutored by the hulking beady-eyed Cheney cannot.

The grown-up cartoon Bush was much slyer: here he is sitting behind a wall with an American soldier in Iraq and telling him, "I know all the talk from the Democrats about sending you home was undercutting morale. So we added three months to your tour, just to cheer you up." It captured the casual brazenness of a man who, visiting soldiers horribly wounded in the war he had badly managed, urged public support for his leadership as a sign of support for the men and women his lousy leadership had put in harm's way. This is a plot worthy of Shakespeare.

Still, it's hard for cartoons to deal with something like the Military Commissions Act that legalized torture, suspended habeas corpus and constructed a loose web of law by which you and I could be hung by our ankles in a meat locker for as long as somebody deemed necessary. "Any person is punishable" the law stated, "who knowingly and intentionally aids an enemy of the United States." And when it comes to deciding what "knowingly and intentionally" might mean or who is the enemy that would be for a military commission to decide in secret, with or without you present. No Fifth Amendment, hearsay evidence admissible, no judicial review. But how do you put that into a cartoon? It's such a Gestapo world the White House tried to establish, but do you draw Mr. Bush in shiny jodhpurs and a monocle, flicking a whip against his boots, a swastika on his lapel? You'd look like a kook if you did, and yet the Military Commissions Act was in fact reminiscent of Germany in 1933, when the Reichstag passed the Enabling Act to give the Chancellor the power of summary arrest and imprisonment.

It's hard to imagine a cartoon George W. Bush with his arms around two urchins labeled POOR and OPPRESSED or doing battle with a hairy monster (TERRORISM) or standing watch over an ivy-covered cottage (MIDDLE CLASS), given what the man has been up to. As the President himself said, "You never know what your history is going to be like until long after you're gone." And right now, with some time left still before he departs the Oval Office, the nation waits eagerly for him to be gone. In his presidential library, he'll be ranked with Lincoln and FDR, but to most of us, he's a man intellectually and temperamentally unequipped to rise to the challenge, rigid, shallow, overwhelmed by events in a world he doesn't dare look around and see. In other words, a small man in a big hat, a six-gun aimed at his foot.

INTRODUCTION
Eight Years of Civility and Respect

Like every other presidential candidate, George W. Bush made lots of promises when he first ran for that almighty office. His promises were vague, as campaign pledges always are; and yet we still remember them as vividly as if he made them yesterday. We recall his promises to govern piously but mercifully as a "compassionate conservative." We remember his clear promises to "bring us together"—Richard Nixon's famous promise on election night in 1968—which Bush reiterated throughout his campaign in 2000, albeit in different words: "I'm a uniter, not a divider."

As a candidate, Bush also made other, more specific promises: to reduce CO_2 emissions "within a reasonable period of time"; to pursue a "humble" foreign policy; to "strengthen Social Security"; to "give every family access to affordable health insurance"; and so on. And while he made such promises overtly and deliberately, Bush also often made another sort of promise. While all his standard campaign promises were tightly crafted, this one was, to say the least, unscripted. Several times a week, and quite by accident, Bush promised that he just might be the funniest of our modern presidents, if not the funniest this nation's ever had. He made this promise not on

purpose, but despite himself—the way that Gerald Ford was funny when he took a tumble down the stairs of *Air Force One*. Or Jimmy Carter, when he tried to pronounce "nuclear." Bush was a fount of wild misstatements, mangled pronunciations, and malapropisms, many of them far more interesting, and entertaining, than anything that he or any other politician said on purpose.

This is not to say that Bush could get laughs only inadvertently. Indeed, throughout the campaign there was vivid evidence that Bush could do hilarious riffs, although his humor might not necessarily please everyone. On the website thesmokinggun.com, for instance, there is a minute of great footage from a wedding video shot in Texas in 1992, in which Bush, big drink in hand, regales his buddies with a cutting (some might call it nasty) and ad-libbed mock-testimonial to the happy couple, demonstrating the irreverent wit that no doubt helped to make him popular at his prep school Phillips Andover and Delta Kappa Epsilon, his fraternity at Yale (as well as, possibly, at Skull & Bones, if they do any laughing there). That video has long remained unknown to most Americans, perhaps because the "liberal media" did not properly appreciate the young man's politically incorrect sense of humor; or perhaps because they did not want Americans to see how much fun Bush could be when evidently tying one on (six years after he'd officially gone on the wagon).

Still, Bush was always at his funniest despite himself. Thus we all (or many of us) laughed at first, when Bush said, for example, "I know how hard it is to put food on your family," or vowed not to let terrorists "hold this nation hostile, or hold our allies hostile," or asked famously, "Is our children learning?" Yet it wasn't quite as funny as it seemed, in part because Bush and his team adroitly turned the comedy to his advantage, casting his weird English as an emblem of backwoods authenticity—a major help to a campaign obsessed with making Master Bush (Yale '68, Harvard '75) come off like Judge Roy Bean. Embracing the tactic, Bush started jesting publicly about his own troubles with the mother tongue, and, later, even provided a friendly blurb for an edition of *Bushisms*, a collection of his finest bloopers ("I'm kind of proud that my words are already in book form"). By the time Will Ferrell was impersonating Bush on *Saturday Night Live* (in a skit titled "Strategery!"), the joke was starting to fall flat, since Bush himself was in on it.

And yet the joke went on—until 9/11 changed the world, and all the laughter died.

Bush, we heard again and again, had found his voice as Anti-Terrorist-in-Chief, and for a year or so he was beyond all criticism. His godlike aura started fading in 2003, however, and he soon resumed the long slow fall that had been underway when those airliners exploded in New York, Pennsylvania, and Washington.

Meanwhile, he kept coming out—and even now keeps coming out—with more accidental gems: "We want results in every classroom so that one single child is left behind," he said in Little Rock on November 10, 2003. In Erie, Pennsylvania, on September 4, 2004, he promised "supplemental funding, which is money for arms and body parts and ammunition and fuel." "I'm looking forward to a good night's sleep on the soil of a friend," he said in Washington on June 29, 2005 (commenting on an upcoming visit to Denmark). "I understand how tough it is, sir. I talk to families who die," he chided a reporter who had asked about the challenges of war, on December 7, 2006. "The stronger the wetlands, the more likely the damage of the hurricanes," he said in New Orleans (or what was left of it) on March 1, 2007. And so on.

Viewed from the twilight of Bush's term, what is most edifying about his gaffes is their predictability: Bush tends to speak in broken English only when the subject doesn't interest him or appears to irk him. Tellingly, he blows it when he tries to improvise about the have-nots ("how hard it is to put food on your family"), education ("Is our children learning?"), the well-being of our troops ("money for arms and body parts"), those bereft by war ("the families who die"), or from dangers either natural ("Save the life who had been affected by Hurricane Katrina!" he said on September 6, 2005) or man-made (those who would "hold this nation hostile"). If the subject is peace or freedom or American democracy, Bush has trouble speaking lucid English off the cuff. By contrast, he tends to have no trouble when his theme is war, revenge, or punishment, and he has no trouble saying "no," putting others down, or flaunting his own powers as he imagines them. "I'm the decider, and I decide what is best." "Bring it on." "Dead or alive. Either way. It doesn't matter to me."

In this way, Bush's speech has always told us clearly, if obliquely, what he and his cohorts are really all about: making the rich richer, and the poor poorer, the prisons bigger, and America more like her own worst enemies. Such policies gradually turned most Americans against him. Today, only a small minority—about one-fifth of us—supports Bush fervently, and some of those only because they revere the office he happens to hold.

The rest of us can see that Bush has long since broken all his early campaign promises, and that it's no laughing matter.

So how did we get into this horrific fix? We can best begin to answer that grave question by reviewing the satiric gems collected here. Aside from their keen comic pleasures (we could all use a laugh, let's face it), these cartoons are invaluable *reminders* at this moment of widespread forgetfulness. At their best, first of all, political cartoons recall those inconvenient truths that tend to disappear too soon from the "official" news, if they come up at all—e.g., that Bush was not elected, that he blew a hefty surplus, failed to properly arm our troops, and named extremists to the federal bench, etc. And thus, more broadly, these cartoons also remind us that American democracy depends on such irreverence from the Fourth Estate; for if our press had properly exposed the doings satirized in these cartoons, we would not be marveling at them now.

Running On Empty

Any candidate facing an incumbent must run a negative campaign. This does not mean that you have to take cheap shots, aim punches at the crotch, fling mud, or even be discourteous. You must "go negative," rather, by hammering at the essential fact that you *are not him* (or *her*). Thus JFK ran as the anti-Eisenhower (young blood, great hair, and, apparently, a healthy heart), Jimmy Carter campaigned as the anti-Nixon ("I will never lie to you"), Ronald Reagan as the anti-Carter (strong and sunny rather than morose and impotent), and so on.

It was therefore no surprise when Bush the Younger ran *around* Al Gore and campaigned as the anti-Clinton—i.e., as a man of *character*. Given Clinton's infamous libido and Bush's socially conservative, pious base, "character" meant simply sexual restraint: Bush would presumably "restore dignity and honor to the White House" by hosing down the furniture and never, ever, taking off his pants. (He also vowed to staff the place with "decent men and women"—solid citizens who, he added vividly, "will not stain the house.") Bush had to tread lightly here, of course, as Clinton's "character" was not so odious to most Americans, who had in fact *supported* him

throughout his inquisition by the Starr chamber. And so the governor breathed not a word about the whole impeachment hoo-ha that had lately split the Congress—and that had also set the stage for his own rise. Rather, he relied on quasi-martial code words like "honor," "decency," "integrity," and "character," which now steamed with salacious innuendo.

It was, or should have been, a risky move for Bush to campaign as a man of character. If character were merely chastity, then Richard Nixon was a man of sterling character, as were Savonarola, Oliver Cromwell, Robespierre, Heinrich Himmler, and Bob Haldeman. "Character," in fact, refers to a complex set of virtues, which—chastity aside (as far as we know)—Bush has never demonstrated. Indeed, many of the defects in *his* character were well-established by the time he ran for president, because of several stories that emerged in 1999.

There was the matter of his spotty military service during the war in Vietnam—a war he supported, but one the young Bush had avoided through a preferential entry into the Texas Air National Guard (TANG). Whereas Dan Quayle had been mauled for doing the same thing in Indiana, Bush's draft-dodging was at first reported in a whisper, and then not at all. There was also Bush's history as a businessman: one bust after another, each of them obligingly cleaned up by wealthy interests eager to do Bush the Elder a big favor; and a fortuitous stock sale that looked rather like insider trading, and whose proceeds Bush then used to buy into the Texas Rangers—a sweet deal that soon made him a multimillionaire. Whether such moves added up to racketeering (the SEC, run by an avid Bush supporter, quickly cleared him) or just dumb luck, it did not reflect well on Bush's character, though it did illustrate the awesome power of his family name. In short, there was an awful lot of real and pertinent dirt on Gov. Bush. The 2000 presidential race was the ideal occasion for it all to come to light. That's not what happened, as these cartoons demonstrate.

By contrast with the furor expended over Quayle's and then Bill Clinton's military service ("feeding frenzy" was the phrase used by the elder Bush in miffed response to Quayle's ordeal) in 1988 and 1992, respectively, Dubya's experience engendered little media coverage and abruptly vanished from the news after December 1999. By and large, the press also ignored the other skeletons in Bush's bursting closet, and even minimized his grim accomplishments as governor of Texas—vast poverty, an endless carnival of executions, toxic fogbanks of pollution—while keeping mum about his kinship with the theocratic right.

Meanwhile, Al Gore pulled his punches. Going for "the high road," he and his campaign were too polite to mention Bush's scandals, and actually played *down* the differences between the two.

Thus *no one* questioned Bush's "character," for all the lip service he paid to this concept, and there was little talk about his possible agenda besides. Instead, most discussion focused on how he and Gore were doing on TV. In that competition both candidates were deemed, conveniently, to be rough equals, thus freeing the press from looking below the surface and analyzing the substantive differences between Bush and Gore. As many of the cartoons here recall, the race apparently was nothing but a televisual contest between two dull personas: the "wooden" Gore ("stiff as a board") against the blockhead Bush ("thick as a plank") (p. 23). The spectacle was so dispiriting that cartoonist Jack Ohman could depict them as simply squalling babies being held by their respective elders, H.W. Bush and Bill Clinton (p. 26).

Justified or not, such cynicism about the seriousness of the campaign worked to Bush's clear advantage. If all that matters is how well your image plays on television, "woodenness" is actually a graver failing than, say, ignorance, irrationality, and heartlessness, which can easily be spun as openness, simplicity, and toughness. Predictably, that is how Bush was sold to the public by his team—and, remarkably, the media largely bought it, casting "Dubya" as a good old boy more natural and authentic than awkward, pedantic Gore. That bias helped the Bush campaign "define" Gore as a spoiled and pompous braggart. As these cartoons remind us, Gore took endless flak not only for his "woodenness" but also for his tendency to "serial exaggeration"—a myth that was itself based on a series of exaggerations and plain lies—and for his sheltered background as a sort of Beltway brat: "Prince Albert" Gore's dad was a *politician*, and the child was raised in a *hotel in Washington*, and schooled in snooty places like St. Albans and Harvard. Karl Rove's soldiers deftly managed to obscure the fact that all these talking points *applied to Bush himself*—for it was *he* who lied repeatedly about his past, *he* who'd grown up in the lap of luxury (his family far wealthier than Gore's), and *he* the child of highly privileged politicians. (While Gore's grandfather was a farmer, Bush's was a power on Wall Street, then a U.S. senator—and a Republican more liberal than Al Gore.)

This corrective view was largely absent from the media coverage of the race, but Bush's long dependence on his family, et al., was not lost on the cartoonists. The toughest sketches in this section represent Bush as a toddler, or a baby monkey, or an imbecile—a hapless little guy without a clue, completely dwarfed by his responsibilities and guided carefully (if grudgingly) by Dick Cheney, Condoleezza Rice, and Colin Powell. Although not flattering, of course, that caricature casts Bush as innocent of any animus or motivation of his own. It is, in fact, a comforting depiction, for it represents him as essentially benign, and his overseers as competent (or capable). It is thus similar to the standard view of Bush's difficulties

8/23/97	1/19/99	12/13/99	2000	8/3/00	9/4/00	11/3/00
Texas Gov. George W. Bush unofficially begins to run for president by attending the GOP Midwestern Leadership Conference in Indianapolis.	Bush begins his second term as governor of Texas. "Still undeclared, Bush says his wife and two daughters are reluctant to support his run for president," CNN reports.	Asked which political philosopher had influenced him most, Bush names Jesus.		At the Republican National Convention in Philadelphia, Bush accepts his party's nomination.	Standing at an open mike, Bush refers to *New York Times* reporter Adam Clymer as "a major-league asshole."	Fox News reports that Bush had been arrested and convicted for drunk driving in Kennebunkport in 1976.

speaking English: a sign of unpretentiousness, as opposed to an alarming inability to speak a lucid sentence on such subjects as peace, education, economic justice, and democracy.

Which brings us to the climax of the year 2000 and of the long (and, so far, largely secret) campaign to make Bush president, despite the will of the electorate. Through the joint efforts of several Florida Republicans (including his brother, Gov. Jeb Bush, and Katherine Harris, Florida's Secretary of State and co-chair of the state's Bush/Cheney campaign),

and, eventually, the Supreme Court, Bush was made to seem to win the race in Florida—where, we later learned, he actually had *lost*. As the consortium that counted up the votes eventually determined (and as the press reported very quietly a few weeks after 9/11), Gore would have won if every ballot in the state had been appropriately counted, even with Ralph Nader in the picture. This was, and is, a shattering fact—a scandal so enormous that the press has largely looked away from it. It is a great relief, however, that this scandal is treated properly in some of these must-see cartoons.

11/7/00	11/8/00	11/19/00	12/8/00	12/12/00	12/23/00
Election Day. The media project a victory for Al Gore in Florida.	Led by Fox News, the media project Bush as the winner in Florida. Gore calls Bush to concede, but then decides against it as the numbers keep fluctuating.	Posing as outraged Floridians, GOP operatives shut down the manual recount of the ballots in Miami-Dade County.	Florida Supreme Court orders a manual recount of disputed ballots throughout the state.	By a vote of 5–4, the Supreme Court halts the Florida recounts, effectively proclaiming Bush the winner.	Bush appoints John Ashcroft as U.S. Attorney General.

Republican candidate Dan Quayle indirectly attacked the credentials of his former boss's son, George W. Bush by saying "I won't need on-the-job-training." Quayle dropped out after coming in eighth in the June 1999 Iowa straw poll and later endorsed Bush.

In February, Sen. John McCain (R-Ariz.) beat Bush in the New Hampshire primary by 49 to 30 percent, respectively.

TWO ITEMS THAT WENT UP FOR SALE AT THE SAME TIME

THE APPALLING VIDEO OF
THE COLUMBINE SHOOTINGS

THE APPALLING GEORGE W.
BUSH, PURCHASED BY THE NRA.

The *Washington Post* reported on May 4 that NRA vice president Kayne Robinson had boasted that "if Republican nominee George W. Bush wins in November, 'we'll have . . . a president where we work out of their office.'"

"I think we ought to raise the age at which juveniles can have a gun."

George W. Bush,
St. Louis debate, 10/17/00

> "I have a different vision of leadership. A leadership is someone who brings people together."
>
> George W. Bush,
> Bartlett, Tenn., 8/18/00

> "I understand small business growth. I was one."
>
> George W. Bush,
> *New York Daily News*, 2/19/00

☆ PRESIDENTIAL TIMBER 2000 ☆

"I understand reality. If you're asking me as the president, would I understand reality. I do."

George W. Bush,
on *Hardball*, 5/31/00

In April, Bush chose Halliburton CEO and former Secretary of Defense Dick Cheney as his running mate. While Republicans pushed Cheney as a fair-minded non-ideologue, Cheney's record in the House of Representatives showed that he voted not just against federal funding of abortions, but also against re-funding the Clean Water Act, against a seven-day waiting-period on handgun purchases, and even against the very creation of the Department of Education.

"Yes, in principle, Bush could win. The stock market could crash. Gore could be caught shagging an intern. Bush could electrify the country with the greatest performance in the history of presidential debates. But barring such a grossly unlikely event, there is no *reason* to think Bush will recover. . . . Stick a fork in him. He's done." —William Saletan on Bush trailing Gore by five points in polling, *Slate*, 9/14/00

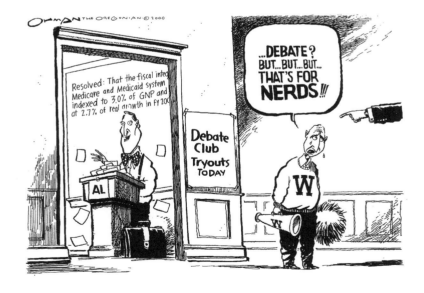

ELECT **GEORGE** BUSH:
THE WISE APPROACH!

SUBLIMINAL AD PAID FOR BY THE
REPUBLICAN NATIONAL COMMITTEE.

On September 12, Bush said he was "convinced" that an ad
placed by the Republican National Committee that flashed
the word "RATS" over a Gore prescription drug proposal was
not at all intended to send a subliminal message. According to
Bush, "We don't need to play cute politics."

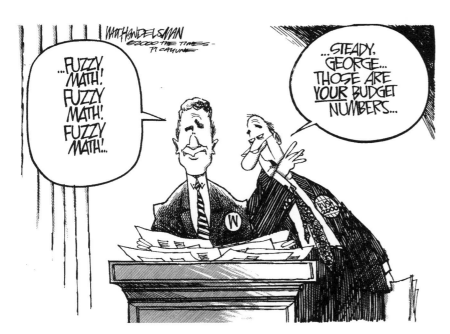

"It's clearly a budget. It's got a lot of numbers in it."

George W. Bush,
Reuters, 5/5/00

"I do know I'm ready for the job. And, if not, that's just the way it goes."

George W. Bush,
Des Moines, Iowa, 8/21/00

"One of the great things about books is sometimes there are some fantastic pictures."

George W. Bush,
U.S. News & World Report, 1/3/00

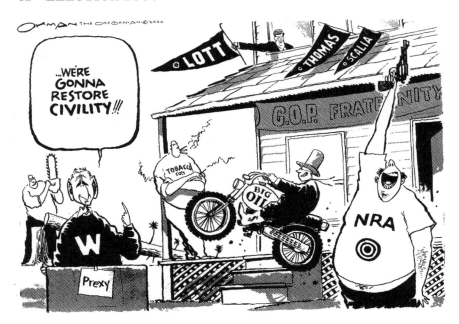

"There are pledges all the time."

George W. Bush,
on breaking his campaign
pledge not to support a sales
tax as governor of Texas,
ABC's *This Week*, 1/23/00

DRIVING UNDER THE INFLUENCE.

According to the Federal Election Commission, Gore received 50,999,897 votes in the popular election, while Bush got 50,456,002; a difference of 543,895 votes. Since Green Party candidate Ralph Nader took in 2,882,955 votes—most of which were assumed to have gone to Gore if Nader had not run—it is a widely held belief that Nader was the "spoiler" in the election who kept Gore from winning.

"I will swear to not, to uphold the laws of the land."

George W. Bush,
Toledo, Ohio, 10/27/00

"I thought how proud I am to be standing up beside my dad. Never did it occur to me that he would become the gist for cartoonists."

George W. Bush,
Newsweek, 2/28/00

"The great thing about America is everybody should vote."

George W. Bush,
Austin, Texas, 12/8/00

"I think we agree, the past is over."

George W. Bush,
Dallas Morning News, 5/10/00

> "The administration I'll bring is a group of men and women who are focused on what's best for America, honest men and women, decent men and women, women who will see service to our country as a great privilege and who will not stain the house."
>
> George W. Bush,
> *Des Moines Register*
> debate, 1/15/00

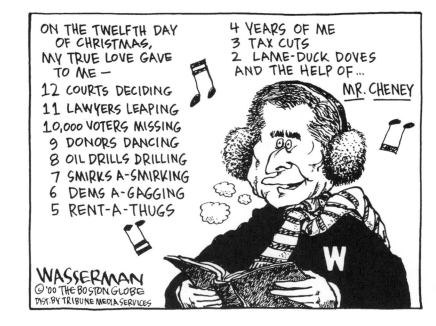

After a baffling post-election battle (the most fractious such controversy since the nineteenth century), capped by a 5–4 U.S. Supreme Court decision on December 10 blocking the manual recount of Florida votes ordered by the state's Supreme Court, Gore conceded to Bush in a televised address on December 13, saying he was doing it "for the sake of our unity of the people and the strength of our democracy."

"America better beware of a candidate who is wiling to stretch reality in order to win points."

George W. Bush,
on his campaign
plane, 9/18/00

"I am mindful of the difference between the executive branch and the legislative branch. I assured all four of these leaders that I know the difference, and that difference is they pass the laws and I execute them."

George W. Bush,
Washington, D.C., 12/18/00

> "They misunderestimated me."
>
> George W. Bush,
> Bentonville, Ark., 11/6/00

"If this were a dictatorship, it would be a heck of a lot easier, just so long as I'm the dictator."

George W. Bush,
Washington, D.C., 12/18/00

From Stooge to Caesar

Bush had a rocky "honeymoon," and it was all down-hill from there. This was not because the Democrats refused to cut him any slack, or because the "liberal media" was out to get him. On the contrary, although Bush had been *installed* as President by five Supreme Court justices on no clear legal grounds, the Democrats caved in as soon as Justice Rehnquist administered the secret handshake on Inauguration Day. There was loud opposition to the tax cut that Bush wanted, John Ashcroft's confirmation hearings threw off lots of sparks, and there were murmurs of a possible resistance to Bush and Cheney's looniest judicial nominees; but on the whole the Democrats were as submissive as St. Paul says wives should be (Ephesians 5:23). They acquiesced in the re-imposition (on January 22) of a global gag order on U.S.-funded international health groups, whose workers now could not even talk about abortion. (While largely feigning moderation on abortion rights throughout the presidential race, at one point Bush had blurted out his true intentions: "If I'm the President," he said in his debate with Al Gore on October 17, "we're going to have gag orders.")

When Bush unveiled his Office of Faith-Based Initiatives on January 29, the Democrats just blinked, while Madison spun in his grave. And, of course, they simply dropped the subject of the President's selection by judicial activists and ignored the evidence of vast election fraud throughout south Florida.

Bush's inauguration was a tense, tumultuous affair—a festival more evocative of Guatemala City than of Washington. The crowd was huge, and loud with disapproval, with protesters popping up all over. You can sense as much from the cartoons in this chapter. Otherwise, you simply had to be there, or wait three years for the release of Michael Moore's *Fahrenheit 911*, with its startling footage of the presidential limo being halted by the mob, then speeding off to safety—less a fit reception for a newly sworn-in president than a lately captured felon.

From that inglorious beginning Bush drifted downward in the polls, as everything his White House did made him still less beloved: his tax policies and budget cuts, his slash-and-burn approach to the environment, Dick Cheney's secret meetings with Enron CEO Ken Lay in April to block regulation of the wholesale energy market, John Ashcroft's sermons, the start of Bush/Cheney's assault on the Occupational Safety and Health Administration, and on and on. Nor was

Bush's slide reversed when, in March, he suddenly and loudly broke off missile talks with North Korea (thereby touching off events that led to the current stand-off with Kim Jong-Il); nor was his slide reversed in April when he thumped his chest at China over the disposition of a U.S. spy plane that had landed on Chinese soil—an adolescent show of toughness (as the cartoon on p. 58 suggests) which served only to exacerbate the crisis, thereby offering an early glimpse of his extraordinary lack of diplomatic finesse.

The year's cartoons remind us that Bush was, at that time, still generally regarded as a mutton-headed puppet, jerked around by other, more nefarious manipulators. Despite the extra-legal measures whereby Bush had taken power—or, perhaps, because of them—the press in general (and many of the rest of us) persisted in the view that he was operating squarely in the mainstream of American political traditions. A few observers—including some of these cartoonists—saw the extremism of Bush's White House. For instance, Matt Davies (pp. 63 and 65) and Walt Handelsman (pp. 60 and 64) captured the administration's special penchant for elitist banditry, with Bush spearheading an attempt to place every civic institution and all our natural resources at the disposal of a global ring of multibillionaires.

Overall, Bush's instincts were neither republican nor democratic but imperial—as he frequently made clear. He had often noted the attractions of autocracy—"If this were a dictatorship, it would be a heck of a lot easier, just so long as I'm the dictator," he had chuckled in 2000—and would do so time and time again. "There ought to be limits to freedom [of expression]," he had snapped on May 21, 1999, riled by a satiric website. In its blunt hostility to all divergent views and awkward questions, the Bush campaign foretold the Bush regime: herding demonstrators into "First Amendment zones," and freezing out reporters who dared broach forbidden subjects.

Bush's military goals were also clear before his swearing-in, despite his campaign promise of a "humble" foreign policy ("I just don't think it's the role of the United States to walk into a country and just say, 'We do it this way, so should you,'" he had said on October 11, 2000). Indeed, there were early signs that Team Bush wanted war and plenty of it. Not least among these signs was the fact that since 1998, the Project for a New American Century (PNAC)—

Dick Cheney was a charter member, in company with a rogue's gallery of other eminent neo-conservatives—had been pushing hard for a pre-emptive war against Saddam Hussein, a policy that Bush endorsed explicitly—and in perfect English—in August 2000. "What if you thought Saddam Hussein, using the absence of inspectors, was close to acquiring a nuclear weapon?" Charlie Rose asked him. "He'd pay a price," Bush replied.

> Rose: What's the price?
> Bush: The price is force, the full force and fury of a reaction.
> Rose: Bombs away?
> Bush: You can just figure that out after it happens.

Such talk went unnoticed, or at least unmentioned, by the press—even after other PNAC stalwarts like Rumsfeld, Richard Perle, and Paul Wolfowitz joined the new administration and started agitating for another war against Iraq. Those large dots went unconnected by the media—even after it was (quietly) reported, ten days before he was inaugurated, that Bush already had his sights set on Saddam: "Iraq is Focal Point As Bush Meets with Joint Chiefs" (*New York Times*, January 11, 2001).

The Democrats and press alike made little of all this, and so Bush came across not as a would-be emperor or warrior but as an incompetent rube in way over his head. By the summer of 2001, he was a standing joke so broad that Letterman and Leno mocked him nightly. There was even a new cable sitcom, *That's My Bush*, that cast the president as a good-hearted halfwit bossed around by that nasty "Mr. Cheney."

But all that changed on 9/11—or rather, 9/12, since Bush's first response to the disaster was to cut and run, to "get out of harm's way," as he ingenuously put it. Once the commander-in-chief returned to the public eye, the fact that he had high-tailed it was quite forgotten—along with everything that most of us had learned about his character. Prostrated by fear, the nation turned toward Bush, thinking—hoping—he

1/20/01	1/22/01	2/1/01	3/8/01	3/28/01	4/4/01	5/16/01	5/24/01
Bush is inaugurated as the nation's 43rd president.	Bush reinstates the "global gag rule" barring U.S. funds for family-planning groups that offer or discuss abortion.	Bush suspends Bill Clinton's ban on road-building and logging in the national forests.	Bush clashes publicly with Kim Dae-jung, the visiting South Korean president, over the latter's rapprochement with Kim Jong-Il of North Korea.	Bush backs out of the Kyoto Protocol on global warming.	Premiere of sitcom *That's My Bush!* on Comedy Central.	Cheney's energy task force calls for weak environmental rules and mammoth subsidies for the oil and gas, coal, and nuclear industries.	Sen. Jim Jeffords (R-Vt.) leaves the GOP, which now loses control of the Senate.

2001

would be the Great White Father that the moment seemed to call for. His approval ratings shot way up: from 50 percent in August to 82 percent by the end of September, according to Zogby.

For the moment, then, it seemed heretical to talk about Bush's, or Cheney's (or Mayor Giuliani's) prior laxness toward the threat of terrorism. Nor did it seem to matter that most experts on terrorism were arguing that 9/11 ought to be regarded as a criminal assault and not an act of war. Cooler heads claimed that Bush's bombs-away response would only give the terrorists exactly what they wanted, but the point was lost. Also lost were many of our fundamental rights as U.S. citizens, when Congress passed the USA PATRIOT (Uniting and Strengthening America by Providing Appropriate Tools Required to Intercept and Obstruct Terrorism) Act on October 26. (The bill passed with few legislators having read it. It was very long and quite complex, and Cheney threatened to denounce as "soft on terrorism" anyone who tried to take the time to study it before the vote.)

Thus, as the year came to a close, Bush became the towering figure that he had obviously always meant to be; and many good Americans were thrilled that Sheriff Bush had come to wipe out every varmint in the world (Dana Summers, p. 78). Millions who had lately snickered at him now revered him as he sat there in the saddle, polishing his badge. At that moment of crisis, the terrified townsfolk forgot that they had wanted someone else to do that job (Davies, p. 57).

6/19/01	8/9/01	9/11/01	9/12/01	10/26/01	11/12/01	11/13/01	12/2/01
Cheney refuses to release the records of his energy task force meetings to the Government Accountability Office.	Bush bans research on new stem cells.	Terrorist attacks on New York and Washington. Bush flies from Florida to Nebraska, to, as he put it, "get out of harm's way."	Bush returns to Washington, arriving at the White House around 7 p.m.	Bush signs USA PATRIOT Act	A long-awaited study of the ballots cast in Florida reveals that Al Gore would have won if all the votes there had been counted.	Bush orders the establishment of military tribunals to try suspected terrorists.	Enron files for bankruptcy

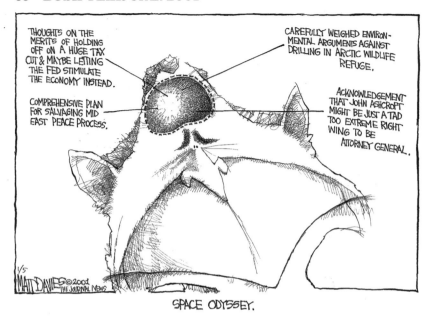

SPACE ODYSSEY.

{ Bush picked former Colorado Attorney General Gale Norton as his Secretary of the Interior. Environmental groups were outraged, given her long history of lobbying for energy interests and her well-demonstrated hostility to environmental regulations.

LAURA BUSH (and student)

"I'm glad the first lady is here. It's an unusual job where all you've got to do is walk down from your living room and come to work. I'm really proud of Laura."

George W. Bush,
Washington, D.C., 2/1/01

> "I do remain confident in Linda [Chavez]. She'll make a fine labor secretary. From what I've read in the press accounts, she's perfectly qualified."
>
> George W. Bush,
> Austin, Texas, 1/8/01

> "If he's—the inference is that somehow he thinks slavery is a—is a noble institution I would—I would strongly reject that assumption—that John Ashcroft is a open-minded, inclusive person."
>
> George W. Bush,
> *NBC Nightly News*, 1/14/01

"I want everybody to hear loud and clear that I'm going to be the president of everybody."

George W. Bush,
Washington, D.C., 1/18/01

"Bush: 'Our Long National Nightmare of Peace and Prosperity is Over.' "

satirical headline from *The Onion*, 1/17/01

> "Then I went for a run with the other dog and just walked. And I started thinking about a lot of things. I was able to—can't remember what it was. Oh, the inaugural speech, started thinking through that."
>
> George W. Bush,
> *U.S. News & World Report*, 1/22/01

> "[John Ashcroft's] unyielding and intemperate positions on many issues raise grave doubts both about how he will interpret the oath he would take as Attorney General to enforce the laws and uphold the Constitution, and about how he will exercise the enormous discretionary power of that office."
>
> Sen. Patrick Leahy (D-Vt.),
> Washington, D.C., 1/29/01

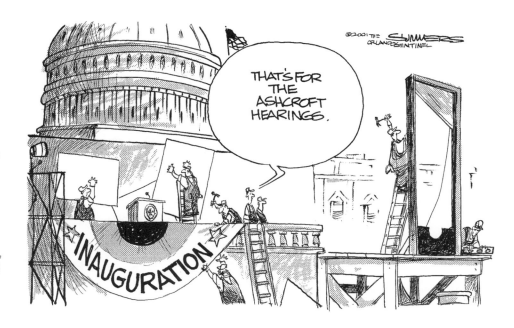

> "The thing that's important for me is to remember what's the most important thing."
>
> George W. Bush,
> St. Louis, 2/2/01

In June, Bush signed into law the first of his sweeping tax cuts. Critics claimed the cuts mostly rewarded the rich, such as billionaire Steve Forbes, who had been pushing a "flat tax" plan for years.

On April 1, a U.S. EP-3 spy plane collided with a Chinese fighter jet in international airspace, killing the fighter pilot and forcing the EP-3 to land in Chinese territory. The American crew of twenty-four was held captive until April 11, after the delivery of a letter of apology from the U.S. government.

"Having slashed funding for clean, new sources of energy, Bush then promises to reinstate it some time in the future—from fees raised on leases for oil drilling in the Arctic National Wildlife Refuge . . . Bush promises to destroy the environment first, in order to raise enough money to try to save it later."

Bill Press,
Tribune Media Services, 4/12/01

In Bush's first 100 days in office, he blocked funds to international family-planning groups offering abortion (Day 3), created a White House office to disburse government funding to religious groups (Day 10), reversed a rule reducing levels of arsenic in drinking water (Day 60), and rejected the Kyoto Protocol on climate change (Day 67).

After Donald Rumsfeld dismissed the 1972 Anti-Ballistic Missile Treaty—a cornerstone of détente policy—as "ancient history," Bush proposed a missile defense system (dubbed "Son of Star Wars"), which many foreign leaders vociferously opposed, believing it would set off a new arms race. In 2007, Bush's proposal for a European missile-defense system further damaged diplomatic relations with Russia.

©2001 Tribune Media Services

www.reuben.org/jones/

BUSH ADVISER KARL ROVE (and boss)

"There's no question that the minute I got elected, the storm clouds on the horizon were getting nearly directly overhead."

George W. Bush, Washington, D.C., 5/11/01

"War is God's way of teaching Americans geography."

Ambrose Bierce

Former oil executives Bush and Dick Cheney were attacked for crafting energy policies that were too industry friendly, to put it mildly. Oil and gas companies gave more to Bush's 2000 campaign than any other federal candidate over the last decade, with $1.8 million in contributions.

"It was amazing I won. I was running against peace and prosperity and incumbency."

George W. Bush,
Gothenburg, Sweden, 6/14/01

In late May, Sen. Jim Jefford (R-Vt.) became an independent, throwing control of the Senate to Democrats for the first time since 1994. Jeffords, a longtime Republican, said he felt he had no choice but to leave the GOP after assessing Bush's fiscal 2002 budget and his plan to overhaul the public education system.

"Conservation may be a sign of personal virtue, but it is not a sufficient basis for a sound, comprehensive energy policy."

Dick Cheney,
USA Today, 5/1/01

"Russia is no longer our enemy and therefore we shouldn't be locked into a Cold War mentality that says we keep the peace by blowing each other up. In my attitude, that's old, that's tired, that's stale."

George W. Bush,
Des Moines, Iowa, 6/8/01

Bush's rejection of the 1997 Kyoto Protocol on climate change (he referred to it as "unrealistic" and questioned the science on greenhouse gases) in the summer of 2001 likely damaged U.S. international relations more than any of his other actions—the term "slap in the face" being frequently employed—that is, until the invasion of Iraq.

> "I suspect that had my dad not been president, he'd be asking the same questions: How'd your meeting go with so-and-so? . . . How did you feel when you stood up in front of the people for the State of Union Address—state of the budget address, whatever you call it."
>
> George W. Bush,
> *Washington Post*, 3/9/01

· The President has tea with the Queen ·

"She was neat."

George W. Bush on
meeting Queen Elizabeth II,
Times of London, 7/18/01

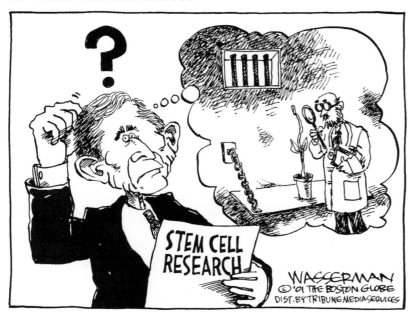

On August 10, Bush agreed to allow extremely limited federal funding of stem cell research, after a battle pitting those believing the research could help cure diseases like Parkinson's and Alzheimer's against pro-life advocates, who considered destroying stem cells akin to taking a human life.

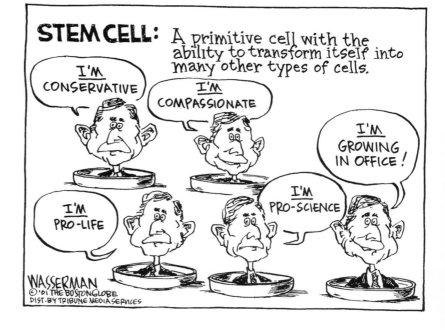

{ In a late August CNN/*USA Today*/Gallup poll, Bush had a 55 percent approval rating, with only 46 percent of respondents saying he deserved reelection. The sharp federal surplus drop was seen as a serious problem by 73 percent, and 72 percent thought Bush was responsible.

"—AND HERE'S WHERE I GO WHEN I WANT TO GET AWAY FROM IT ALL!..."

{ After much debate, on August 3, the House passed a bill allowing oil drilling in Alaska's Arctic National Wildlife Refuge—it was a crucial component of Bush's energy policy.

"SIR, I REALLY THINK WE SHOULD BE LOOKING AT A LONGER-TERM SOLUTION!"

"As I'm sure you can imagine, it is an unimaginable honor to live here."

George W. Bush,
Washington, D.C., 6/18/01

"Nobody can threaten this country. Oh, they may be able to bomb buildings and obviously disrupt lives."

George W. Bush,
Washington, D.C., 9/20/01

On January 25, 2000, Condoleeza Rice received a memo from Richard Clarke (Counterterrorism Coordinator, National Security Council) declaring "we urgently need" to brief the FBI, CIA, State, and Defense departments on al Qaeda. That meeting didn't happen until September 4. In early summer, Clarke asked to be transferred, frustrated by an administration he considered not "serious about al Qaeda."

GROWTH SPURT

"We are fully committed to working with both sides to bring the level of terror down to an acceptable level for both."

George W. Bush,
Washington, D.C., 10/2/01

"When I was a kid I remember that they used to put out there in the Old West a wanted poster. It said, Wanted: Dead or Alive."

George W. Bush,
Washington, D.C., 9/17/01

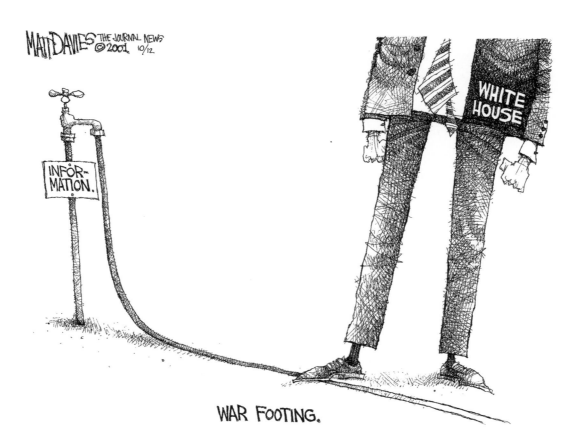

WAR FOOTING.

"You know, it's the old glass box at the—at the gas station, where you're using those little things trying to pick up the prize, and you can't find it. It's—and it's all these arms are going down in there, and so you keep dropping it and picking it up again and moving it, but—some of you are probably too young to remember those—those glass boxes, but—but they used to have them at all the gas stations when I was a kid."

Donald Rumsfeld, The Pentagon, 12/6/01

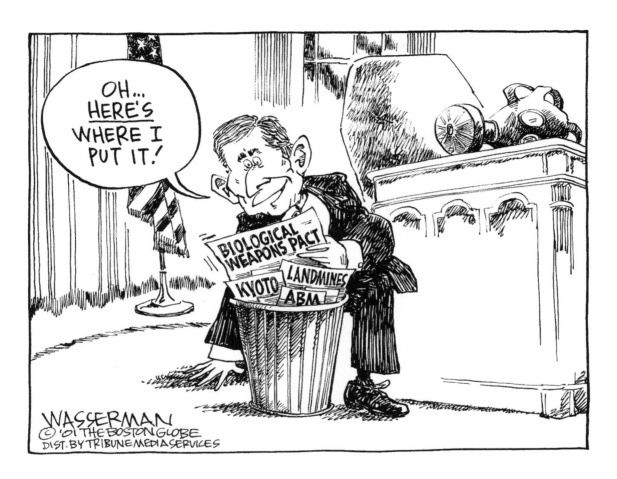

"First, we would not accept a treaty that would not have
been ratified, nor a treaty that I thought made sense for
the country."

George W. Bush,
referring to the Kyoto Protocol,
Washington Post, 4/24/01

In late 2001, Bush and Russian President Vladimir Putin began strengthening ties in the name of fighting terrorism. As a result, U.S. rhetoric regarding Russian human rights abuses in its widely condemned campaign in Chechnya was toned down.

"We need to counter the shockwave of the evildoer by having individual rate cuts accelerated and by thinking about tax rebates."

George W. Bush,
Washington, D.C., 10/4/01

George Augustus

Although a dark time for the rest of us, 2002 was clearly Bush's favorite year; the whole world was now his stage, and he was free to act upon it as "a war president." The role agreed with him, to say the least. All year Bush was walking tall, and looking good—and speaking lucid English, as long as he avoided subjects other than the "war on terror." Whenever he strayed off the battleground, he would either accidentally tell the truth ("We need an energy bill that encourages consumption"), utter sheer nonsense ("The goals for this country are a compassionate American for every single citizen"), or make two contradictory claims at once (as when he addressed the need "to restore chaos and order in Iraq," or when, attempting to sound like a man of peace, he declared "I will use our military as a last resort, and our first resort").

With few exceptions (and despite the efforts of the nation's editorial cartoonists), no one was laughing now: the Young Pretender had been magically replaced by George Augustus, and that new leader spoke about his regal power with a clarity that was a lot more troubling than his flights of gibberish. "I'm the commander," he told Bob Woodward in the summer. "See, I don't need to explain—I do not need to explain why I say things."

"There's only one person who is responsible for making that decision, and that's me," he said to Barbara Walters on December 13, on the subject of the—or, rather, his—upcoming war against Iraq. A few weeks later, when a reporter asked him about "the possibility of war looming in Iraq," Bush said, "You said we're headed to war in Iraq. I don't know why you say that. I hope we're not headed to war in Iraq. I'm the person who gets to decide, not you." Such imperial remarks expressed the same mad narcissism that had marked his State of the Union speech on January 29, when he had infamously vowed to purify Iraq, Iran, and North Korea, aka the "Axis of Evil." The speech wasn't so much an update on where we were as a country (as the constitution mandates) as it was a chilling recitation of the neo-conservative agenda for remaking the world and realigning the economy according to their ideological dictums.

At such moments, Bush spoke not just from the heart but wholly in the spirit of his government, which, thanks to the USA PATRIOT Act, was becoming, more and more, an extension of the White House—a White

House, moreover, that was now devoted mainly to political activism of the kind that Richard Nixon had once made notorious, although Nixon was as mellow as the Grateful Dead by contrast with John Ashcroft and his deputies. Perceiving a world of enemies, the White House started cracking down on all of them at once, trampling civil liberties at home and human rights abroad with unprecedented zest (and very little media coverage). Countless immigrants were hauled off for interrogation or detention and innumerable citizens placed under surveillance. Meanwhile, the U.S. government was sweeping up suspected "terrorists" and shipping them to places like Guantanamo (and others less well-known), where they were often tortured—ostensibly interrogated—by U.S. officials, military and civilian. In cases of "extraordinary rendition," the torturers were foreign nationals, or, reportedly, private "contractors" employed by U.S. paramilitary corporations.

All such measures were, of course, defended as essential to "homeland security," while anyone who criticized them publicly was accused of terrorism, too. As Bush put it succinctly on January 5, "There are no shades of gray. Either you're with the United States of America or you're against the United States of America." Thus, Ashcroft warned civil libertarians: "To those who scare peace-loving people with phantoms of lost liberty, my message is this: Your tactics only aid terrorists, for they erode our national unity and diminish our resolve." Such statements might have sounded less like empty bullying if Ashcroft's sweeps had rounded up a single proven terrorist.

For that matter, it would have been a little easier to buy the administration's nonstop warning of "another 9/11" if they had shown the slightest interest in uncovering the truth about the first one. Certainly there are some crackpot theories on that subject, but none of them is as bizarre as Bush and Cheney's efforts to *prevent* a full investigation.

That counter-drive began in January. When the Democrats announced their plans for a congressional inquiry, Cheney made several phone calls to Tom Daschle, then Senate Majority Leader, ordering him *not* to broaden the investigation beyond the failures of the FBI and CIA, and *not* to make it public, or the White House would cast Daschle and his colleagues as Islamist stooges. Once the Joint Select Committee set to work a few weeks later, the White House further blocked its work by holding back key documents. By the summer, that sort of treatment—and, more important, the rising public clamor by survivors of those killed on 9/11—had pushed many Democrats, and some Republicans, to call for an independent new commission.

At first, Bush and Cheney lobbied Congress not to vote for the 9/11 Commission; and then, after claiming on June 6 to support it after all, they quietly continued to thwart it through a series of obstructive tricks, and to limit its effectiveness as much as possible. By the time it started holding hearings in 2003, the commission had just eighteen months to complete its work, limited subpoena power, and a budget of $3 million. (In comparison, the budget for the *Challenger* commission had been $50 million, while Whitewater finally cost some $60 million.) Once the body finally got to work, or tried to, the White House kept impeding it, delaying security clearances for some commissioners, withholding countless documents, and refusing interviews.

While thus blocking the full story of the terrorist attacks, the White House took no real precautions to prevent or mitigate "another 9/11." Throughout 2002 (and after), Bush did nothing to enhance security for U.S. ports, trucks, highways, tunnels, nuclear plants, or petrochemical facilities. Nor, amazingly, was there much real improvement in the security at U.S. airports. (Meanwhile, Bush did spend additional millions on missile defense, and on the mass surveillance of Americans.) Such protective measures mattered far less to the administration than laying the groundwork for the war that Bush and his team had been pushing for, discreetly, from the start.

A year after 9/11, CBS reported that, within a few hours of the terrorist attacks, Donald Rumsfeld told his posse in the Pentagon to link the horror to Saddam Hussein. "Go massive," he said, in ordering the search for "evidence" of some connection to Iraq. "Sweep it all up. Things related and not." The next year was devoted mainly to selling that fiction, although the sales team took care not to spotlight their disinformation drive until the fall. "From a marketing point of view, you don't introduce new products in August," Andrew Card, Bush's chief of staff, told *The New York Times* on September 6.

1/8/02	1/11/02	1/16/02	2/14/02	5/6/02	6/1/02	7/15/02
No Child Left Behind Act signed into law.	First Afghan prisoners arrive at Guantanamo.	Rep. Henry Waxman (D-Calif.) reveals that Enron heavily influenced Cheney's energy task force report.	White House announces "Clear Skies," a program that will actually delay reduction of three major air pollutants.	Bush pulls out of the treaty to create an International Criminal Court.	In a speech at West Point, Bush proclaims the "Bush Doctrine" of preemptive war.	Government starts Operation TIPS, urging meter readers, telephone repairmen, cable installers, and other U.S. workers to report "suspicious" doings in private homes.

2002

When the time was right, the hucksters started up in earnest, crying hard throughout the media for war against Iraq, and hinting loudly that Saddam Hussein had somehow been involved in 9/11 and was just months (weeks? days?) away from nuking the United States. "We don't want the smoking gun to be a mushroom cloud," warned Condoleezza Rice, then–national security adviser, on CNN's *Late Edition* on September 8. Their "case" was finally nothing more than a farrago of big lies and intense hallucinations, including dark tales of "aluminum tubes" that could be used in "centrifuges," a momentous rendezvous in Prague between Mohammad Atta and a mysterious Ba'athist officer, and, crucially, Saddam's sly purchase of "significant quantities" of yellowcake uranium in Niger. Whether Bush et al. were lying to themselves as well as to the rest of us, their scare tactics surely helped distract attention from a host of issues that the White House would prefer we all ignore (and which are listed by Don Wright on p. 112).

All that flimflam about Saddam made big news (and those who questioned it, like WMD expert Scott Ritter, were tuned out, smeared, or ridiculed). Quietly, meanwhile, Bush, Cheney, and their men were busy setting up a vast surveillance system meant to monitor all seven continents. In January, the Pentagon established the Information Awareness Office, whose mission was to "imagine, develop, apply, integrate, demonstrate, and transition information technologies, components and prototype, closed-loop, information systems that will counter asymmetric threats by achieving *total information awareness*" (emphasis added). And in November, Bush signed the Homeland Security Act, creating the Department of Homeland Security (see Drew Sheneman, p. 100, for a diagram). Then sometime later in the year, Bush signed a secret presidential order formalizing the National Security Agency's illegal warrantless surveillance of Americans on U.S. soil—a program that had started quietly a few weeks after 9/11. Through such stealthy measures the White House set its sights not merely on the world's "terrorist parasites" (a quasi-Maoist epithet that Bush had used in his State of the Union speech) but on We the People.

8/26/02	9/5/02	10/29/02	11/5/02	11/25/02	11/27/02	12/6/02	12/12/02
Cheney claims that Saddam Hussein could have nuclear weapons "fairly soon."	White House announces "Healthy Forests," a program that will open old-growth forests to commercial loggers.	Bush signs the Help America Vote Act, which radically extends the use of electronic voting machines.	Election Day. Republicans win upset victories in Georgia, Colorado, Minnesota, and New Hampshire.	Homeland Security Act signed into law.	Bush names Henry Kissinger to chair the 9/11 Commission.	Treasury Secretary Paul O'Neill and economic adviser Lawrence Lindsay.	Bush dismisses Bush signs executive order to permit federal funding of religious groups.

"And so, in my State of the—my State of the Union—or state—my speech to the nation, whatever you want to call it, speech to the nation—I asked Americans to give 4,000 years–4,000 hours over the next—the rest of your life—of service to America. That's what I asked—4,000 hours."

George W. Bush,
Bridgeport, Conn., 4/9/02

SHENEMAN The Star-Ledger · Tribune Media

"TSK TSK PLAYING AROUND WITH PEOPLE'S RETIREMENT MONEY! FOR SHAME, FOR SHAME."

Texas energy giant Enron (whose CEO Kenneth Lay personally contributed over $600,000 to Bush's political career) collapsed in a massive accounting scandal in late 2001. Soon after, it was alleged that Dick Cheney had tried the previous summer to collect on a massive debt allegedly owed to Enron from politicians in India. The administration maintained Enron enjoyed "no special favors," even though an April 2001 memo from Lay to Cheney was almost entirely replicated in the White House's energy policy.

In Bush's first State of the Union address, on January 29, he infamously termed North Korea, Iraq, and Iran "an axis of evil." Clinton's Secretary of State Warren Christopher later termed this resonant turn of phrase "A speech-writer's dream and a policy-maker's nightmare."

"There's nothing more deep than recognizing Israel's right to exist. That's the most deep thought of all. . . . I can't think of anything more deep than that right."

George W. Bush,
Washington, D.C., 3/13/02

"I've been to war. I've raised twins. If I had a choice, I'd rather go to war."

George W. Bush,
Charleston, W.Va., 1/27/02

"What is your ambitions?"

George W. Bush,
to students at Parkview
Arts and Science Magnet School,
Little Rock, Ark., 8/29/02

"The invisible part of everything that you thought you could see, you can't see."

George W. Bush
on the Palestinian-Israeli conflict,
Crawford, Texas, 4/4/02

EARTH DAY PRESENT

"Mine is a results-oriented administration. When we say we expect results, we mean it."

George W. Bush's
Earth Day address, 4/22/02

Already famously hostile toward international agreements, the Bush administration in 2002 fought to have the International Criminal Court Treaty include an exemption for U.S. personnel, claiming foreign nations would use the ICC to legally harass members of the military serving overseas. On May 6, the U.S. formally withdrew from the treaty, making it the only state still actively fighting the ICC—except Libya.

In May, Jimmy Carter visited Cuba and met with Fidel Castro. Besides criticizing the country's lack of freedoms on Cuban TV, Carter also called for the U.S. to lift travel and trade restrictions. Bush's policy, however—developed with help from right-wing Cuban-Americans—held the hardline approach, even though critics noted the United States had more restrictions on dealings with Cuba than with Iraq or China.

"This foreign policy stuff is a little frustrating."

George W. Bush,
New York Daily News, 4/23/02

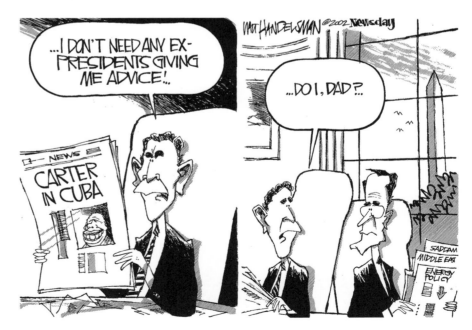

> "We've got a vast coalition of nations that are still with us. They heard the message, either you're with us, or you're not with us. They're still with us."
>
> George W. Bush,
> Washington, D.C., 5/14/02

"BEAT THE DRUM LOUDER, CONDI! THESE EUROPEANS MUST BE DEAF!"

{ Bush started his first European tour on May 22, primarily to enlist more help in combating terrorism, particularly to include Iraq in the so-called "War on Terror." Polls showed that support among Europeans for America and fighting terror, which had been very high after 9/11, had almost melted away by this point, as Europeans worried that the "Axis of Evil" rhetoric would drag them into a vaguely defined and interminable global conflict.

"As we know, there are known knowns. There are things we know we know. We also know there are known unknowns. That is to say we know there are some things we do not know. But there are also unknown unknowns, the ones we don't know we don't know."

Donald Rumsfeld, Dept. of Defense news briefing, 2/12/02

"I just want you to know that, when we talk about war, we're really talking about peace."

George W. Bush,
Washington, D.C., 6/18/02

In late June, after the exposure of massive accounting fraud at
WorldCom, Bush called on Congress to pass his corporate responsibility plan. Meanwhile, there were continual revelations about
Bush's 1990 sale of stock from Harken Energy (where he was a
director at the time), which many charged was insider trading.
Though Bush was cleared by the SEC, doubts lingered about the
president's ability to lecture on corporate responsibility.

"That characterization is so far from the mark that I am shocked—sort of."

Donald Rumsfeld,
Washington, D.C., 3/28/02

"Corporate malfeance [sic] has had an effect on our economy and we need to do something about it."

George W. Bush,
Waterford, Mich., 10/14/02

> "Sometimes when I sleep at night I think of [Dr. Seuss'] *Hop on Pop*."
>
> George W. Bush,
> Pennsylvania State
> University, 4/2/02

IT DIDN'T LOOK ANY BETTER ON DUKAKIS.

"Sometimes things aren't exactly black and white when it comes to accounting procedures."

George W. Bush
about his old oil firm,
Washington, D.C., 7/8/02

"When one of us suffer, all of us suffers."

George W. Bush,
addressing Pennsylvania
coal miners, 8/6/02

GEORGE W. BUSH

"August was a month of accomplishment here in Washington."

George W. Bush,
Washington, D.C., 8/2/02

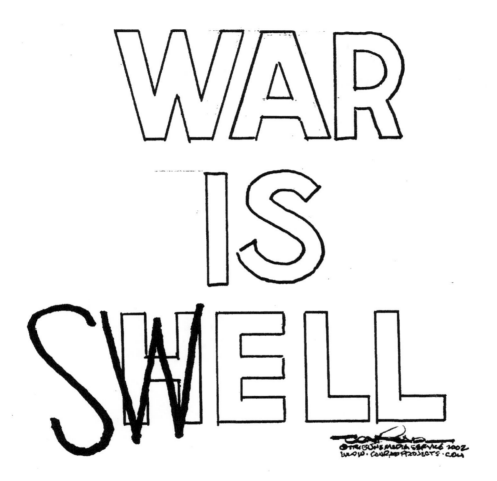

"See, we love—we love freedom. That's what they didn't understand. They hate things; we love things. They act out of hatred; we don't seek revenge, we seek justice out of love."

George W. Bush,
Oklahoma City, 8/29/02

In August, in preparation for a likely invasion of Iraq, Bush met with Saudi ambassador (and close family friend) Prince Bandar to try to persuade his country to support attacking Iraq, just as they had during the First Gulf War. The meeting was not successful. A Saudi foreign policy adviser later told CNN, "There is no country in the world that I know of that supports military action against Iraq at this time."

"[Iraq is] an enormous country. You know, it's bigger than Texas, or as big, I guess. I haven't looked lately."

Donald Rumsfeld,
Washington, D.C., 12/23/02

"If I know the answer, I'll tell you the answer, and if I don't I'll just respond, cleverly."

Donald Rumsfeld,
Bagram Air Base, Afghanistan, 4/27/02

> "We haven't heard much from him. And I wouldn't necessarily say he's at the center of any command structure. And again, I don't know where he is. . . . I truly am not that concerned about him."
>
> George W. Bush,
> discussing Osama Bin Laden
> during a news conference,
> Washington, D.C., 3/13/02

> "The goals for this country are peace in the world."
>
> George W. Bush,
> Washington, D.C., 12/19/02

On October 10 and 11, the House and Senate voted overwhelmingly in favor of a resolution authorizing President Bush to use military force against Iraq if Hussein refused to give up his WMDs as dictated by the United Nations.

jackass
the war

"There's an old saying in Tennessee . . . that says, Fool me once, shame on—shame on you. Fool me—you can't get fooled again."

George W. Bush,
Nashville, 9/17/02

"There's no bigger task than protecting the homeland of our country."

George W. Bush,
Stockton, Calif., 8/23/02

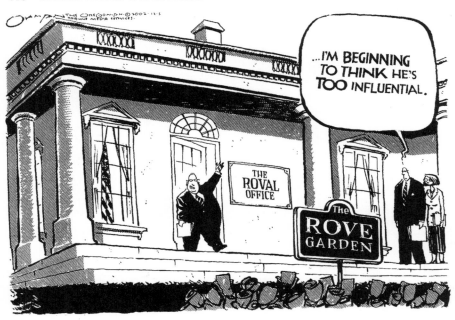

"We have an advantage here in America—we can feed ourselves."

George W. Bush,
Stockton, Calif., 8/23/02

"Job creation and economic security, as well as homeland security, are the two most important priorities we face."

George W. Bush,
Washington, D.C., 11/7/02

"UNFORTUNATELY, AL GORE'S NOT THE 'GHOST OF ELECTIONS PAST'
I GOTTA WORRY ABOUT!..."

In early December, Sen. Trent Lott (R.-Miss.)—speaking at a
100th birthday celebration for Strom Thurmond—appeared to
endorse Thurmond's virulently pro-segregation fight during the
Civil Rights Era. Apologies couldn't quell the firestorm and on
December 20, Lott stepped down as Senate Majority Leader.

"I don't think [invading Iraq] would be that tough a fight."

Dick Cheney,
Meet the Press, 9/8/02

Hard Sell

Two thousand three was a mixed year for Bush. Yes, he and his people finally got their war, which started on March 20. That was an amazing feat, considering there were no grounds for it, and that millions of people from around the world had raised their collective voice against it, on February 15, in the largest global protest on record, including mammoth demonstrations in 150 cities throughout the United States. Even that "slam dunk" of a war could not, however, reverse the long, slow fall of Bush's star, which was soon descending as it had been prior to 9/11. From early February into May, the president's approval ratings rallied one last time, starting with the Space Shuttle *Columbia* disaster (a horror that re-traumatized the nation) and continuing through the fall of Baghdad and the dramatic toppling of Saddam Hussein's statue in Firdos Square on April 9.

The high point of those giddy weeks came on May 1, when Bush, dressed as a Navy pilot, disembarked from a fighter jet on the deck of the USS *Abraham Lincoln*, the former Air National Guardsman thereby fostering the illusion that he had just pulled off a tricky carrier landing ("Yes, I flew it," he told the press). Then, having changed into his civvies, Bush announced to all the world: "Major combat operations in Iraq have ended"—a proclamation hammered home by the proud words, "MISSION ACCOMPLISHED," inscribed mightily across a massive banner hung behind him. Hours earlier, Defense Secretary Donald Rumsfeld had declared the war was over in Afghanistan. Few suspected that both claims were premature ejaculations (so to speak); for, in reality, "major combat operations" in both countries were just getting started.

Aside from its deceptiveness, that show aboard the *Lincoln* was a staggering display of the wrong stuff. As the carrier was only 30 miles from San Diego, Bush could have boarded far more easily by helicopter; but so modest an arrival would have yielded no hot visuals. "If you looked at the TV picture," one aide said later, "you saw there was flattering light on his left cheek and slight shadowing on his right. It looked great." To get that shot, the *Lincoln* had to be diverted from its course, which kept all those sailors and Marines—who had been away from home for months—at sea for one more day. The cost for this charade? An extra $3.3 million—slightly more than the whole budget for the 9/11 Commission. Such details went largely unreported by the media, some of whose leading men and women gushed embarrassingly over the theatrics of Bush's *Top Gun* moment. ("Tom Cruise! Look at him!" shrieked CNN's Kyra Phillips.) For the editorial cartoonists, of course, the "Fly Boy Photo Op" presented multiple opportunities for comment, both in 2003 (David Horsey, p. 141) and beyond (Dan Wasserman, p. 310).

By and large, the U.S. media kept kowtowing to the president throughout the year (and the year after). We the People, however, were less reverent. There were now so many Americans entangled in the "war on terror" overseas that certain facts were getting out despite the press's mainly upbeat coverage. A lot of people therefore knew, for instance, that some of the soldiers posted to Iraq were "mentally unfit," as the manpower shortage forced the Pentagon to lower standards (as UPI reported in mid-March). People knew that troops were forced to drive unarmored Humvees (as *Newsweek* reported briefly on May 3) and given defective body armor (as the AP reported in October). People knew that troops, in the infernal summer of Iraq, were short on water, and that Cheney's Halliburton had been serving them contaminated

meals (as NBC belatedly reported in December). And people knew the Pentagon cut hazardous duty pay for those fighting in Iraq (in August), slashed veteran's benefits (in November), shut schools and commissaries on military bases nationwide (throughout the fall), and charged hospitalized troops for meals, while those flying home on leave were stuck for part of their own airfare. (These last two practices were outlawed by Congress in October.)

Thus by November, the public had so dark a view of Bush's war that some members of the press finally began to pick apart the tripe concocted by the White House and Department of Defense. On *ABC Primetime* on November 11, Diane Sawyer interviewed Jessica Lynch, who disavowed the propaganda tale by which the Pentagon had glamorized her capture and release in Baghdad. And when Bush paid his "surprise" Thanksgiving visit to a unit stationed in Iraq, hoisting a big roasted turkey, the military's own *Stars and Stripes* exposed the calculation of the scene. Some major newspapers reported that the troops included in the feast were all pre-screened, while many others had been turned away, and that the turkey was a decorative item, not for eating.

Even so, such journalistic "disrespect" was rare, and timid when it did occur. The media never did make clear that Bush was just a passenger aboard that fighter jet, or that the seemingly grand toppling of that statue was actually a propaganda set-up managed by Marines, with a small "Iraqi crowd" bused in for the occasion. Other, larger disappointments also went largely unreported. Conditions in Guantanamo made lots of news—abroad, online, and in the independent press. (The horrors at Abu Ghraib would therefore come as that much more of a surprise in the United States.)

And, while always quick to note Islamist zealotry, the press steered clear of the administration's own fanaticism, such as when, on June 23, Bush told Palestinian prime minister Mahmoud Abbas that, "God told me to strike at al Qaeda, and I struck them, and then he instructed me to strike at Saddam, which I did, and now I am determined to solve the problem in the Middle East." First reported in *Ha'aretz* in Israel, that alarming statement was noted only by a few stateside columnists.

Meanwhile, Bush's government was also cracking down right here at home. On April 7, police attacked nonviolent protestors in Oakland, and "preemptively" arrested more than ninety peaceful demonstrators in Manhattan. In late November, there was a near-blackout on the grim news from Miami, where the latest "free trade" summit meeting had convened, and where some 8,000 people came to protest peaceably. The cops responded with extraordinary violence. With tanks and helicopters out in force, they hit the crowds repeatedly with rubber bullets fired at point-blank range, tear gas, pepper spray, and ear-splitting concussion grenades; and they used stun guns with abandon. (Many activists had stayed away, scared off by the FBI and local cops, who came to question them at home about their plans and views and patriotism.)

Although carried out by Florida police, this was a federal operation, costing $8.5 million, the funds taken directly from the White House's $87 billion budget for the "war on terror" in Iraq. There were other signs of an ambitious militarization of domestic law

	1/29/03	2/5/03	2/15/03	3/20/03	4/9/03	4/10/03	4/11/03	4/12/03	4/12/03	5/1/03
2003	Bush claims that Saddam Hussein "recently sought significant quantities of uranium from Africa."	Secretary of State Colin Powell urges the UN Security Council to approve preemptive war against Iraq.	Largest coordinated antiwar protest ever occurs worldwide in some 800 cities, opposing the invasion of Iraq.	"Operation Iraqi Freedom" starts with air attacks on Baghdad.	Fall of Baghdad. U.S. Marines topple statue of Saddam Hussein in Firdos Square. Rioting, looting start throughout Iraq.	National Museum of Iraq ransacked by looters.	"The medical system in Baghdad has virtually collapsed," announces the Red Cross.	"Stuff happens," says Defense Secretary Rumsfeld.	Congress agrees to spend $79 billion on the war in, and reconstruction of, Iraq.	"Mission Accomplished."

enforcement, including the ever-broadening surveillance of U.S. citizens. In August, the Pentagon set up a new "domestic law enforcement database," and embraced a new "domestic 'data mining' mission"—projects reported by William Arkin in *The Los Angeles Times*, and then mentioned nowhere else.

As the year ground on, and the press began to find its voice again, more and more of us began to get the picture. On July 6, Joseph Wilson published his momentous op-ed in *The New York Times*, revealing that that infamous Niger/Iraq yellow-cake uranium transaction had been fiction. It was also reported that, even as his war grew ever bloodier, Bush devoted all his time to fund-raising, attending not a single military funeral. Californians learned that Bush's Department of Justice was suing to abort the state's tough new clean air standards. Oregonians learned about Ashcroft's

effort to revoke the state's law on assisted suicide. Texans learned that the Republicans had forcibly redistricted their state to suit the party's purposes (and that Tom DeLay had used the Department of Homeland Security to bring state Democrats in line). And people everywhere could see from Bush's latest budget just how "compassionate" he really was: providing still more tax cuts to the rich while further jacking up the national debt, and also establishing the Medicare drug coverage boondoggle, all of which proved quite a gift to the cartoonists in this chapter (Horsey, p. 127, and Drew Sheneman, pp. 128 and 130). Thus Bush's political vital signs kept getting weaker, no matter how carefully his team of spin-doctors tried to manage the arterial flow of bad news from the White House and everywhere in the world where U.S. influence is felt.

7/6/03	7/14/03	7/22/03	7/24/03	8/9/03	9/7/03	10/21/03	11/23/03	12/13/03
Joseph Wilson's op-ed, "What I Didn't Find in Africa," is published in *The New York Times*.	Robert Novak's column outs Valerie Plame, Joseph Wilson's wife, as a CIA agent.	Saddam Hussein's sons, Uday and Qusay, are killed by U.S. forces, and their corpses put on display.	Congressional report on 9/11 released, with section on Saudi Arabia deleted by the White House.	EPA inspector general says White House pressured EPA to minimize health risks from WTC collapse.	Bush asks Congress for an additional $87 billion for the Iraq war.	Congress passes partial-birth abortion ban.	FBI admits to spying on anti-war activists.	U.S. soldiers arrest Saddam Hussein.

"The war on terror involves Saddam Hussein because of the
nature of Saddam Hussein, the history of Saddam Hussein,
and his willingness to terrorize himself."

George W. Bush,
Grand Rapids, Mich., 1/29/03

On January 16, Bush called the University of Michigan's affirmative action plan "fundamentally flawed." Some thought the statement poorly timed, given that the GOP was trying to win African-American voters, and it had been less than a month since Trent Lott had been accused of supporting segregation.

"THIS WOULD GO A LOT SMOOTHER IF YOU'D STOP HUMMING THE THEME TO FINAL JEOPARDY."

"We will, of course, win militarily, if we have to."

George W. Bush,
Washington, D.C., 1/30/03

"I think what you'll find is whatever it is we do substantively, there will be near perfect clarity as to what it is. And it will be known, and it will be known to the Congress, and it will be known to you, probably before we decide it. But it will be known."

Donald Rumsfeld, Washington, D.C., 2/28/03

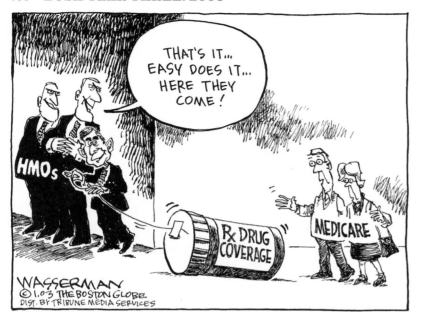

In his 2003 State of the Union address, Bush made reforming Medicare's prescription drug coverage a top priority. Critics quickly assailed the plan as confusing, unhelpful, and quite possibly nothing more than a thinly veiled handout to pharmaceutical companies and HMOs.

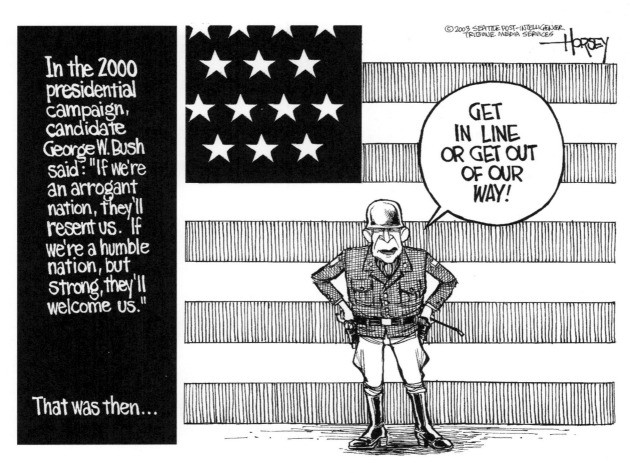

"The game is over."

George W. Bush, discussing
Colin Powell's UN
address about disarming
Saddam Hussein,
Washington, D.C., 2/6/03

In 2003, Bush proposed hundreds of billions of dollars in additional tax cuts that were passed by the legislature, even with the looming threat of war and a record deficit nearing $500 billion.

"I really do believe we will be greeted [in Iraq] as liberators."
Dick Cheney, *Meet the Press*, 3/16/03

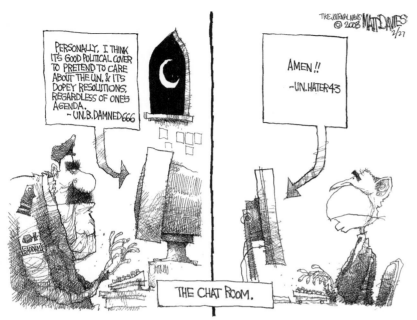

On February 17, Saudi Foreign Minister Prince Saud al-Faisal warned that a unilateral invasion of Iraq would destabilize the entire region. "If change of regime comes with the destruction of Iraq," he said, "then you are solving one problem and creating five more problems."

PRICE TAG FOR IRAQ WAR: $9,000,000,000,000

HUMAN SHIELD

"We're dealing with a country [Iraq] that can really finance its own reconstruction, and relatively soon."

Deputy Sec. of Defense Paul Wolfowitz testifying to Congress, 3/27/03

In early 2003, British Prime Minister Tony Blair's unwavering support of U.S. military action against Iraq—which led him to be called "Bush's poodle," among other, less charitable things—was backed by only 19 percent of Britons.

"I'm the master of low expectations."

George W. Bush,
on *Air Force One*, 6/4/03

Given Cheney's ties to oil and contracting monolith Halliburton, charges of favoritism and war profiteering were heard soon after the company was handed a massive, no-bid contract for reconstruction work in Iraq.

"Freedom's untidy, and free people are free to make mistakes and commit crimes and do bad things. They're also free to live their lives and do wonderful things."

Donald Rumsfeld,
Washington, D.C., 4/11/03

"I think war is a dangerous place."

George W. Bush,
Washington, D.C., 5/7/03

The administration's lone environmental advocate, EPA administrator Christie Todd Whitman, announced her resignation on May 21. Whitman's book *It's My Party, Too*, published in January 2005, charged hard-right extremists with hijacking the Republican Party and losing sight of basic conservative values.

Over two months after the invasion, no stockpiles of WMDs had been found. On May 30, the commander of the 1st Marine Expeditionary Force said, "Believe me, it's not for lack of trying. We've been to virtually every ammunition-supply point between the Kuwaiti border and Baghdad, and they're simply not there."

"Security is the essential roadblock to achieving the road map to peace."

George W. Bush,
Washington, D.C., 7/25/03

SHENEMAN The Star-Ledger - Tribune Media Services

"ONE LAST THING BEFORE YOU GO. THIS PASSAGE, 'GLOBAL WARMING CAN BE ATTRIBUTED TO RISING CONCENTRATIONS OF SMOKESTACK AND TAILPIPE EMISSIONS.' LET'S CHANGE 'SMOKESTACK AND TAILPIPE EMISSIONS' TO 'SOLAR PANELS'".

On June 19, CBS News reported that a huge government report on the state of the environment had been heavily edited by the administration, over protests by EPA staffers. Strongly worded phrases about climate change and its human causes were either deleted or watered down; in at least one case, new material was added from a study partly paid for by the oil industry.

"The world is peaceful and free."

George W. Bush,
Chicago, 6/11/03

"Almost all of the top Bush fundraisers are in the top 1 percent of the nation's incomes [and consequently] are among those who benefit the most from administration legislation reducing the top income tax rate, the capital gains rate and the elimination of taxation on dividend income."

The Washington Post, 7/14/03

Swept under the robe...

In late July, the White House classified part of a 9/11 congressional report allegedly linking Saudi Arabia with al Qaeda. Saudi ambassador Prince Bandar called for declassification, saying, "Saudi Arabia has nothing to hide. We can deal with questions in public, but we cannot respond to blank pages."

An August 22 EPA report showed that some of the agency's news releases about post-9/11 New York air quality downplayed potential problems, primarily due to the influence of the White House Council on Environmental Quality, which convinced the EPA "to add reassuring statements and delete cautionary ones."

"You know, the budgeting process is one that's ongoing.
It's an iterative process, I guess is the best way to put it.
[To Rumsfeld] Iterative is the right word, you think?"

George W. Bush,
Crawford, Tex., 8/8/03

"The first time I met Bush 43 . . . two things became clear. One, he didn't know very much. The other was that he had the confidence to ask questions that revealed he didn't know very much."

Foreign policy advisor Richard Perle, quoted by Sam Tanenhaus in *Vanity Fair*, July 2003

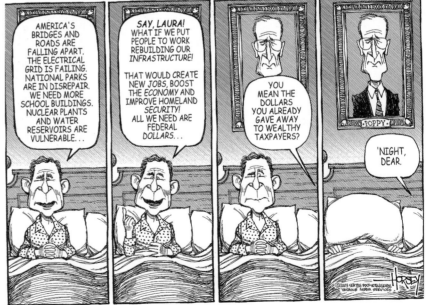

On September 23, Bush addressed the UN Security Council, stressing the correctness of invading Iraq, and asking for member nations to help in reconstructing the nation.

"Just watch."

George W. Bush, answering a reporter's question about how he could spend $170 million on a primary campaign where he was running unopposed, 7/30/03

{ Some of the first serious Democratic opposition to Bush came in late 2003, in response to his extremely conservative choices for judicial nominees. According to one academic analysis, Bush's nominees were as a whole more conservative than those chosen by any modern president, including Nixon, Reagan, and Bush's father.

As the war dragged on, Bush and his supporters criticized the media for focusing on the negative. In November, a member of the conservative Media Research Center said, "There was a point a few months ago when the only news we were getting out of Iraq was bad news." The MRC further claimed that positive news from the more peaceful regions of Iraq went entirely unreported.

"You're free. And freedom is beautiful. And, you know, it will take time to restore chaos and order—order out of chaos. But we will."

George W. Bush,
Washington, D.C., 4/13/03

> "I rarely read the stories, and get briefed by people who are . . . probably read the news themselves."
>
> George W. Bush,
> interview with Fox News, 9/21/03

"I did misspeak . . . We never had any evidence that [Hussein] had acquired a nuclear weapon."

Dick Cheney, *Meet the Press*, 9/14/03

"That's just the nature of democracy. Sometimes pure politics enters into the rhetoric."

George W. Bush,
Crawford, Tex., 8/8/03

"What's the difference?"

George W. Bush,
on whether Saddam Hussein
possessed WMDs or merely
desired them, 12/16/03

Swift Boat to Abu Ghraib

Although the mainstream press continued to go easy on him, Bush had his worst year yet in 2004. From January through Election Day, the news was always bad, and it kept getting worse. Throughout those ten long months there were no triumphs, foreign or domestic, to offset the horror stories, and so Bush kept sinking in the polls—right up until his startling re-election on the evening of November 2.

January had been a month of ugly stories on the war, extinguishing the little glow that Bush got from the mid-December capture of Saddam Hussein. Most shocking was the news from Abu Ghraib, accompanied by photographs of Iraqis bound and tortured by the very soldiers sent to "liberate" them from such treatment by the Ba'athists. There was also troubling news about the White House's case for war. On January 26, two days after resigning as Bush's top weapons inspector in Iraq, David Kay announced his failure to discover any trace of all the hidden weapons of mass destruction (WMDs) that the Bush administration had charged Saddam Hussein with stockpiling: "I don't think they exist," Kay stated flatly on NPR.

Meanwhile, former Treasury Secretary Paul O'Neill—forced to resign in December 2002 for his public questioning of Bush's tax cuts—hit the talk show circuit with a sobering account of his White House experience. In Ron Suskind's *The Price of Loyalty*, O'Neill described a president fixated on Saddam Hussein's removal from the get-go. Only ten days after his inauguration—eight months *before* 9/11—Bush was already gunning for Iraq. "It was all about finding a way to do it," O'Neill told CBS. "The president saying, 'Go find me a way to do this.'" O'Neill also noted Bush's managerial vacuity. Obsessed with war, the president did not respond when faced with other business— "like a blind man in a roomful of deaf people" during Cabinet meetings (see Walt Handelsman, p. 164, and Matt Davies, p. 176), and, one-on-one, completely "disengaged."

While the White House shrugged off the atrocities at Abu Ghraib—the rogue crimes of "a few bad apples," said the president—and whistled past the Kay Report, Team Bush put on their hobnail boots and jumped all over Paul O'Neill: a loose nut, an opportunist, and a liar, they hinted. Even the Treasury Department went after him, ostensibly for leaking classified documents. His ordeal was not unusual, of course, as Bush and Rove had always punished those who told forbidden truths. Now, however, such foul play consumed the White House, as this was an election year, and Bush was running *only* on his image as Our Hero in the "war on terror" (Drew Sheneman, p. 173, and Don Wright, p. 174). It was therefore crucial to discredit anyone who dared to cast a shadow on that image, as O'Neill had done.

In March, Bush's golden helmet was severely dented by another ex-insider: Richard Clarke, who had been counter-terrorism czar under Clinton and then Bush until he quit in protest in 2003. In his bombshell of a book, *Against All Enemies*, Clarke cast Bush *et al.* as stubbornly indifferent to the threat of terrorism prior to 9/11. "I find it outrageous that the president is running for re-election on the grounds that he's done such great things about terrorism. He ignored it," stated Clarke in a *60 Minutes* interview. He also reported that, right after 9/11, Bush had tacitly commanded him to look for evidence connecting the attacks to Iraq. Clarke searched for it, found no such link, and then submitted a report—which was rejected, as it didn't say what Bush (and Cheney) wished to hear.

The regime's negligence made still more news. On April 8, National Security Advisor Condoleeza Rice testified combatively before the 9/11 Commission, arguing that Bush could not have known about bin Laden's plans to attack inside the United States, despite the fact that those plans had in fact been the subject of the Presidential Daily Briefing on August 6, 2001. Rice's effort fizzled when Commissioner Richard Ben-Veniste asked her to repeat the title of that briefing: "I believe the title was, 'Bin Laden Determined to Attack Inside the United States,'" she conceded testily. On April 29, Bush and Cheney themselves testified: conjointly, only once, behind closed doors, with neither of them under oath, and with no transcript (see p. 178 for Chan Lowe's take, channeling Señor Wences, on this testimony). To top it off, the White House reserved the right to censor the commissioners' handwritten notes.

Such moves diminished Bush's stature as the Holy Warrior of 9/11—as did renewed attention to his military "service," which looked even worse by contrast with Democratic presidential candidate John Kerry's bravery in Vietnam. As ever, Team Bush sought to distract attention from the president's unheroic past by slandering others. First, they trashed Kerry's war record through the "Swift Boat Veterans for Truth," one of a variety of "nonpartisan" political groups (so-called 527s) specially created to circumvent recent campaign finance regulations. Given unduly serious consideration by the media at the time (and later found by the FEC to have violated election law), the Swift Boat Veterans was actually a political assault vehicle financed by wealthy Bush backer Sam Fox (now U.S. ambassador to Belgium) and managed by the legendary campaign propagandist Arthur Finkelstein, who had worked for Nixon, Reagan, Al D'Amato, George Pataki, Jesse Helms, and many other not-so-moderate Republicans, and in doing so made the word "liberal" an obscenity. Meanwhile, as Election Day approached, the White House nastily attacked its detractors, including John Edwards (described as "the Breck girl"), Teresa Heinz Kerry, diplomat Joseph Wilson, George Soros, Barbra Streisand, Michael Moore, and many others, while also hyping the enormous "threat" posed by gay marriage to secure the votes of the religious right (as Handelsman, Chan Lowe, and Doug Marlette note on pp. 171 and 172).

The White House then killed off the ever-worsening story of Bush's dubious service in the National Guard by turning it into a referendum on CBS news anchor Dan Rather. In reporting on the issue Rather quoted documents that turned out to be partly bogus—a lapse in judgment that led to his forced departure from the network in November. This journalistic blunder neutralized the bigger issue of the president's true military past, which was now abandoned by the mainstream media (if not by cartoonists like Drew Sheneman, p. 186, and David Horsey, p. 189). Thus Bush dodged that big bullet once again.

At the same time, the administration used all sorts of ways to shut off criticism and pre-empt dissent. Various reports were buried until "after the election": the long-awaited CIA report on 9/11, a damning appraisal of the Bush administration by the U.S. Commission on Civil Rights, and even Bush's annual physical examination were all quietly deferred. The Bush Republicans aggressively policed campaign events, barring or ejecting anyone who was or might look like a Democrat, and sometimes using force to stifle protest. Thus the scene at the Republican National Convention, in New York in late August 2004, was reminiscent of the 1968 Democratic convention in Chicago, with Michael Bloomberg's NYPD spying on activists well in advance of the event, infiltrating

1/5/04	1/22/04	2/18/04	3/24/04	4/13/04	4/28/04	5/4/04	6/5/04
With his energy task force case before the Supreme Court, Cheney goes duck hunting with Justice Antonin Scalia.	Alaska's North Slope opened to oil drilling.	Sixty leading U.S. scientists charge the Bush administration with "misrepresenting and suppressing scientific knowledge for political purposes."	At the Radio and Television Correspondents' dinner, Bush jokes about not finding WMDs in Iraq.	At a press conference, Bush can't think of any errors that he might have made since 9/11.	Images of torture from Abu Ghraib prison first shown on U.S. television.	"Swift Boat Veterans for Truth" air their first TV commercial.	Ronald Reagan dies at 93.

2004

dissident groups, and arbitrarily busting, fingerprint-ing, and detaining more than 1,500 people—nonviolent demonstrators and mere bystanders, who were held for hours, even days, in toxic squalor at Pier 57, quickly dubbed "Guantanamo on the Hudson."

All such nasty anti-democratic theater finally did Bush very little good, as his popularity kept plummeting, among Republicans along with everybody else. It may have been the war, the economy (three million jobs lost, a huge trade deficit, and whopping national debt), the president's Napoleonic attitude, or his pro-business stand on immigration. Whatever caused it, there was growing disaffection on the right. Top Republicans like Bob Barr, John Eisenhower, Gen. Tony McPeak, Francis Fukuyama, and Doug Bandow of the Cato Institute all publicly urged people *not* to vote for Bush. Sixty newspapers that had endorsed Bush four years earlier refused to back him now (with forty backing Kerry, and the others None of the Above). Kerry was the choice of *The Economist* and *The Financial Times*. On October 4, moreover, the latter and *The New York Times* both ran an open letter signed by 169 tenured and emeritus business professors from the world's top business schools, savaging Bush's economic policies,

and formally endorsing Kerry. The letter was con-ceived and drafted by the faculty at Harvard Business School, where Bush had earned his MBA.

And so, despite his badly flawed campaign, Kerry led Bush on Election Day—the odds-makers in Vegas *and* on Wall Street said that he would soon be president-elect. However, on the evening of November 2, Bush won the contest after all, with a slim margin of victory in Ohio, and unexpectedly strong support in many other states. That countless e-voting machines went wrong only in Democratic precincts (with those gadgets mostly manufactured and maintained by Diebold and ES&S, two big private firms with close connections to the GOP), and that countless Democrats could not cast votes because there was no record of their registration, that exit polls predicted *Kerry's* victory by five million votes (Bush won by three million), and that the Bush Republicans resorted to disinformation and intimidation tactics nationwide, were all facts that both the Democratic Party and the press chose largely to ignore (while the cartoonists—like Don Wright, on p. 194, and Taylor Jones, on p. 197—duly noted it). Thus Bush would stay in power for four more years.

6/22/04	6/28/04	7/8/04	7/22/04	8/30/04	11/2/04	11/10/04
On the Senate floor, Cheney tells Sen. Patrick Leahy to "go fuck yourself."	Supreme Court partly restores the habeas corpus rights of "enemy combatants."	Citing the possibility of terrorist attacks, Homeland Security Secretary Tom Ridge asks the Department of Justice about the legal steps required to postpone the election in November.	The *9/11 Commission Report* is published, stating definitely the lack of credible evidence linking Saddam Hussein to 9/11.	Republican National Convention opens in New York, with the sign of the cross clearly visible on the front of the main podium onstage.	Against all odds, Bush and Cheney win re-election.	Bush names Alberto Gonzales as his Attorney General.

{ In January, Paul O'Neill, fired as treasury secretary in December 2002 for frequent disagreements with Bush on his tax cut plans, was quoted in Ron Suskind's book *The Price of Loyalty* (and in the media) alleging that Bush was not only dangerously disconnected from his work, but that his administration had been planning to remove Hussein from power practically from the moment they entered the White House.

"GIVE ME YOUR TIRED, YOUR POOR, YOUR HUDDLED MASSES YEARNING TO MOW LAWNS AND VOTE REPUBLICAN..."

"Then you wake up at the high school level and find out that the illiteracy level of our children are appalling."

George W. Bush,
Washington, D.C., 1/23/04

OHHH, THE STATE OF THAAT UNION...

★U.S.★
- DEFICIT
- ECONOMY
- HEALTH CARE

$1.5 BILLION TO PROMOTE MARRI-AGE.

"There is no such thing necessarily in a dictatorial regime of iron-clad absolutely solid evidence. The evidence I had was the best possible evidence that he had a weapon."

George W. Bush,
Meet the Press, 2/8/04

{ David Kay, the head of the Iraq Survey Group (which led the search for WMDs) resigned on January 23, saying he didn't think they existed. "What everyone was talking about is stockpiles produced after the end of the last (1991) Gulf War, and I don't think there was a large-scale production program in the nineties." On February 3, Bush announced a presidential commission to review intelligence regarding WMDs.

"These stories are being written every day in America. Every single day this is happening. We never hear half of them or any—I never, but, you know—I barely hear any of them, but I just know they're happening."

George W. Bush, in reference to the power of faith in God to cure drug addiction, at a faith-based initiatives conference, Los Angeles, 3/3/04

"Look at these different places around the world where there's been tremendous death and destruction because killers kill."

George W. Bush,
Washington, D.C., 1/29/04

"Twice during his [National] Guard service . . . Bush signed documents pledging to meet training commitments or face a punitive call-up to active duty. He didn't meet the commitments, or face the punishment, [his military records] show."

Boston Globe, 9/8/04

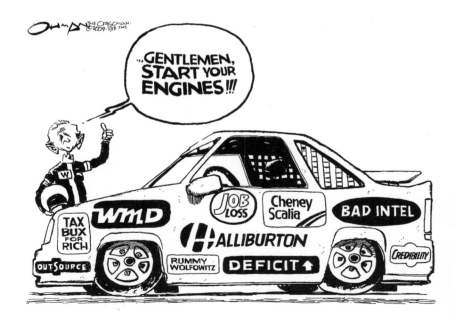

On February 25, Bush announced his support of a constitutional amendment banning same-sex marriages. However, Bush left open the possibility that states could legalize civil unions, angering some of the same social conservatives he was seen as trying to placate with the amendment in the first place.

"We must do what is legally necessary to defend the sanctity of marriage."

George W. Bush,
Washington, D.C., 2/6/04

Bush's reelection campaign was charged with exploitation after running a TV ad campaign that included 9/11 footage of firefighters and a flag-wrapped body being pulled from Ground Zero. Relatives of 9/11 victims called the ads "sick" and "a slap in the face."

"I don't do nuance."

George W. Bush,
Time, 2/15/04

"Recession means that people's incomes, at the employer level, are going down, basically, relative to costs, people are getting laid off."

George W. Bush,
Washington, D.C., 2/19/04

During the 9/11 Commission's hearings, the chance of any connections between Saddam Hussein and 9/11 were explicitly denied. Chairman Thomas Kean later said, "[the evidence] just isn't there."

CONDOLEEZZA RICE and GEORGE W. BUSH

"A free Iraq will be a major defeat in the cause of freedom."

George W. Bush,
Charlotte, N.C., 4/5/04

"NEVER MIND *BIN LADEN* — HAVE YOU FOUND ANY MORE DIRT ON *RICHARD CLARKE?*"

"[WMDs] could still be hidden, like the fifty tons of mustard gas in a turkey farm."

George W. Bush,
Washington, D.C., 4/13/04

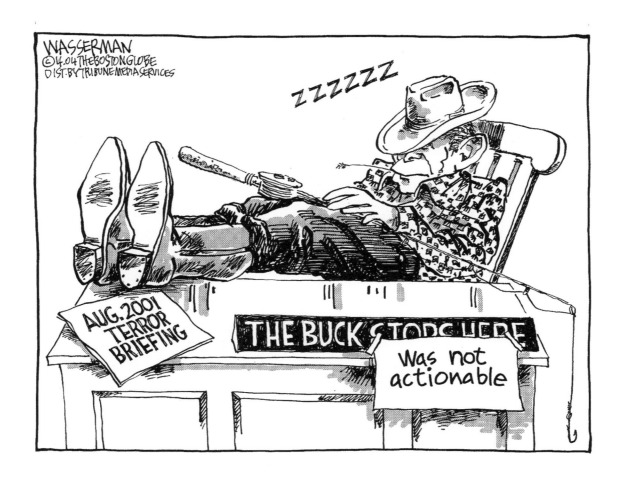

"My job is to, like, think beyond the immediate."

George W. Bush,
Washington, D.C., 4/21/04

FULL METAL BOOK JACKET

{ Two bestselling books made headlines in spring 2004—Bob Woodward's *Plan of Attack* and former counterrorism czar Richard Clarke's *Against All Enemies*—for sharply critiquing Bush's handling of the war on terror and the invasion of Iraq.

"You are a strong secretary of defense and our nation owes you a debt of gratitude."

George W. Bush,
to Rumsfeld at the Pentagon
after the Senate called for
an investigation into the Abu Ghraib
scandal, Washington, D.C., 5/10/04

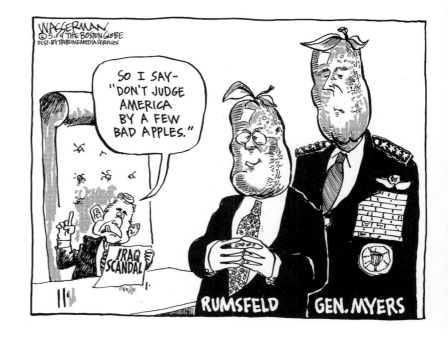

"With the president stepping forward [and endorsing the same-sex marriage ban], this will energize people in a very powerful way."

Tony Perkins, president of the conservative Family Research Council, *The New York Times*, 2/25/04

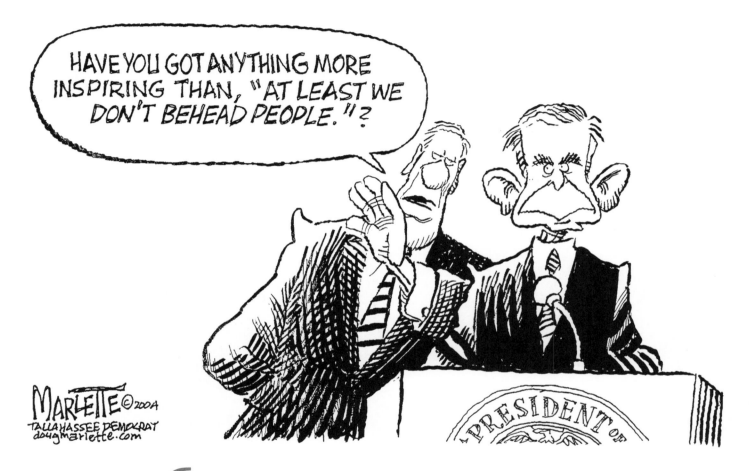

Throughout April and May, the revelation—first reported
by Seymour Hersh in the *New Yorker*—that U.S. forces had
been frequently torturing and humiliating Iraqi captives at
Abu Ghraib prison, would seriously undermine the Bush
administration's attempts to claim the moral high ground
during the conflict.

"It's amazing with the software that has been developed these days that enable a camera to distinguish the difference between a squirrel and a bomb."

George W. Bush,
Washington, D.C., 6/24/04

"American counterterrorism officials, citing what they call 'alarming' intelligence about a possible al Qaeda strike inside the United States this fall, are reviewing a proposal that could allow for the postponement of the November presidential election in the event of such an attack."

Newsweek, 7/19/04

The Associated Press reported on July 22 that a roadside bomb killed a U.S. soldier, north of Baghdad, marking the nine hundredth American military fatality in Iraq since the war began in March 2003.

"That's why I cut the taxes on everybody. I didn't cut them. The Congress cut them. I asked them to cut them."

George W. Bush,
Washington, D.C., 8/6/04

In 2004 the anti-Kerry "Swift Boat Veterans for Truth" group launched a campaign charging him with falsifying his war record, among other things. Although the administration denied any connection, in August Bush's campaign counsel Ben Ginsberg resigned after revelations that he had also been advising the Swift Boat group.

"[Bush's] public records paint a portrait of a Guardsman who, with the cooperation of his Texas Air National Guard superiors, simply flouted regulation after regulation . . . indifferent to his signed obligation to serve."

Eric Boehlert, *Salon.com*, 9/20/04

"Our enemies are innovative and resourceful, and so are we. They never stop thinking about new ways to harm our country and our people, and neither do we."

George W. Bush,
Washington, D.C., 8/5/04

U.S. SECURITY CHECKLIST

CAPTURE BIN LADEN........................ ☐

DISMANTLE AL-QAIDA...................... ☐

HALT N. KOREA NUKE PROGRAM.. ☐

HALT IRAN NUKE PROGRAM.......... ☐

STABILIZE IRAQ .... ☐

DEPORT CAT STEVENS .... ☑

> **I FEEL SAFER ALREADY!**

" I hope you leave here and walk out
and say, 'What did he say?' "

George W. Bush,
Beaverton, Ore., 8/13/04

SHENEMAN TheStar-Ledger TribuneMediaServices

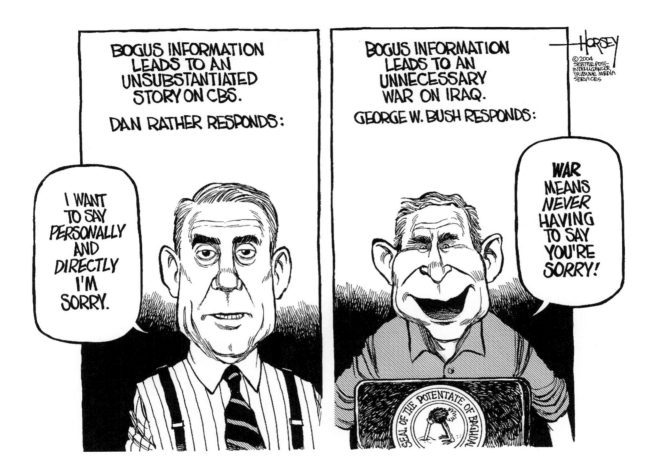

In September, after reporting a controversial *60 Minutes* story alleging that Bush received preferential treatment during his time in the National Guard (charges based in part on documents which were later revealed to be inauthentic), veteran CBS anchor Dan Rather was forced to resign.

"Free societies are hopeful societies. And free societies will be allies against these hateful few who have no conscience, who kill at the whim of a hat."

George W. Bush,
Washington, D.C., 9/17/04

"When no weapons of mass destruction were found in Iraq, Bush shifted his war justification to one of liberating Iraqis from a brutal ruler. After Saddam's capture in December 2003, the rationale became helping to spread democracy through the Middle East."

Tom Raum,
Associated Press, 10/14/06

Photos taken of Bush in the third presidential debate appeared to show a bulge under the back of his suit jacket, prompting some (including a leading NASA scientist and photo analyst) to charge that he had been wearing some form of assisting device, possibly a radio transmitter or receiver.

"It's very important for the American president to mean what he says. . . . That's why I try to be as clearly as I can."

George W. Bush,
Washington, D.C., 9/23/04

FLORIDA
AFRICAN-AMERICAN
VOTING PRECINCT

{ Not long before election day, stories surfaced that the Florida GOP had allegedly compiled secret lists of minority voters to challenge and intimidate at the voting booth.

"I hear there's rumors on the Internets that we're going to have a draft."

George W. Bush,
second presidential debate,
in St. Louis, 10/8/04

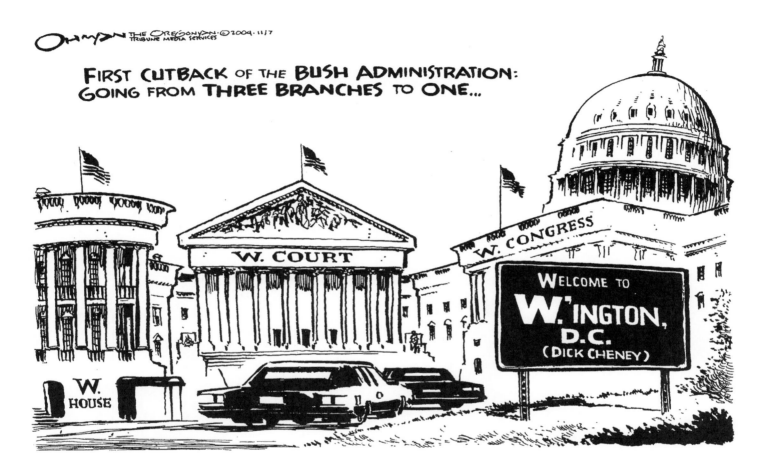

"Fuck yourself."
Dick Cheney to Sen. Patrick Leahy (D-Vt.)
during a photo session,
Washington, D.C., 6/22/04

"In last week's debate, Bush's solution for the most pressing domestic problems of his Presidency was a kind of verbal shrug. . . . According to Bush's philosophy of government, America's ability to assert its will for the greater good around the world is enormous. In Toledo [Ohio]—well, there are limits."

George Packer,
The New Yorker, 10/25/04

GEORGE W. BUSH

"September the 4th, 2001, I stood in the ruins of the Twin Towers. It's a day I will never forget."

George W. Bush,
Marlton, N.J., 10/18/04

A Heck of a Job

Right after the 2004 election, Bush boasted of his "mandate" in financial terms: "I earned capital in the campaign, political capital, and now I intend to spend it," he told the world. That sounded true to most people, as the vast "irregularities" attending Bush's win would not be publicly discussed until much later. Given, then, that Bush most likely "earned" *no* "capital" in the 2004 election, and may in fact have suffered a net loss in support, his "fall" throughout 2005 should be interpreted, perhaps, not as a sudden dip but just the latest phase in his long, gradual decline from late 2002 (as Jack Ohman shows on p. 218).

In any case, 2005 was the year that Bush's chickens started flocking home, as Americans began to see quite clearly what he and his regime were all about. It was the year of no return—the year when all the lies and failures had now finally piled so high that no sane and disinterested person could deny them.

Bush began 2005 by ramping up his drive to "strengthen"—that is, privatize—Social Security, a plan that Americans liked less and less the more they heard him try to sell it. His futile push—intended to shirk the government's responsibility to dues-paying retirees by making them invest their Social Security money in "private investment accounts"—ground on for months, to growing opposition. And yet that drive was not as big a turn-off as the stunt that he, his brother Jeb, and the Republicans in Congress pulled in March, when they tried "saving" the comatose Terri Schiavo, endeavoring to block her husband's efforts to remove her life support through special (and illegal) legislation and a lot of pious bellowing about "judicial murder."

So fervent was the president's desire to meddle in that tragic private matter that he actually cut short the latest of his countless holidays in Crawford, Texas, returning to D.C. to sign the legislation in the wee hours of March 21. It was quite a spectacle, considering the Bush Republicans' eternal promise to protect "the family" against "big government." This may be why the episode demonstrably offended most Americans, self-described conservatives included.

The regime lurched on throughout the spring and summer, lying wildly, hurling mud, and pushing horrible ideas: trashing the Kyoto Protocol, drilling in the Arctic National Wildlife Refuge in Alaska, blocking funds for stem cell research, rolling back rules against road-building in national forests, handing the ticklish job of United Nations ambassador to the ham-fisted

John Bolton even as America grew still more hated globally because of what was happening in Iraq. That all such measures were unpopular both here and elsewhere evidently did not matter in the least. Indeed, it seemed that Bush and Cheney *liked* to give the people what the people didn't want.

Bush also seemed incapable of recognizing the dishonesty and malice in his own behavior, always lashing out at others for the very sins that he and his deputies themselves had been committing on a massive scale. In May, Bush called indignantly on *Newsweek* to retract its claim that a Koran had been flushed down a toilet at Guantanamo. (*Newsweek* complied.) It was striking, first of all, that Bush disputed only one detail in the long exposé of horrors in that gulag—where, it was reported in July, U.S. personnel had first tried out the torture techniques later used at Abu Ghraib. What made the shot at *Newsweek* far more notable, however, was Bush's own disastrous history of canards, including Saddam's legendary secret purchase of uranium (a bit of hypocrisy scored by Matt Davies on p. 213).

Meanwhile, the Valerie Plame affair continued slowly to unravel. In July, Karl Rove was implicated as the mastermind in the criminal campaign to blow the CIA agent's cover in 2003. Here was still more bald duplicity: Bush had been solemnly condemning "leaks" for months—and had lately, and explicitly, vowed to punish anyone involved in Plame's exposure. Now, faced with evidence of an administration member doing exactly that, Bush just sat there, blinking, as in Jack Ohman's cartoon on p. 231.

That Bush's war drive was a pack of lies became clear in May, when *The Sunday Times* (UK) published the explosive "Downing Street Memo," which contained the minutes from a July 2002 meeting of several of Blair's senior ministers. In the minutes, Richard Dearlove, head of MI6 (the British equivalent of the CIA), told Tony Blair quite plainly that "[t]he intelligence and facts were being fixed [by the U.S.] around the policy" of taking out Saddam Hussein. This revelation didn't faze the White House, which kept on venting fantasies in public. (The Iraq insurgency, said Cheney on June 20, is "in the last throes.") The White House's long estrangement from the truth about the war took something of a comic turn in August, when antiwar activist Cindy Sheehan, whose son Casey had died in Iraq, encamped near Bush's Crawford spread in the hope that she might have a word with him—a possibility that kept the brave commander under self-imposed house arrest (David Horsey, p. 220).

But the worst of the regime's domestic failures—in fact, one of the worst in American history—was yet to come. On August 29, Hurricane Katrina slammed into Louisiana and Mississippi, killing untold thousands and devastating a wide swath of the Gulf Coast, particularly New Orleans. It was, in part, a hideous reprise of 9/11, for here again the White House was repeatedly forewarned, and yet did nothing to prevent or lessen the disaster; and here again Bush stayed away. Although FEMA director Michael Brown had warned him that the government was not prepared for "a catastrophe within a catastrophe," Bush spent that day on other matters: chatting with Homeland Security Secretary Michael Chertoff about illegal immigration, sharing birthday cake with John McCain, and pushing his Medicare drug plan at a senior center in Rancho Cucamonga, California. Meanwhile, the levees had broken, the winds had ripped holes in the ceiling of the Superdome where thousands were now cowering, and the Red Cross had announced "the largest mobilization of resources in its history" to help Katrina's victims.

Later, under heavy secrecy (several journalists reported having guns drawn on them by police), the regime quickly searched the ruined neighborhoods and carted off the corpses, leaving a devastated community with no way to compute the number of dead. (FEMA had sealed off the worst-hit areas and impounded cameras, while CNN and others went to court and forced the government to lift its ban on coverage of body recovery efforts.)

Ultimately, Bush's government provided nothing but big talk and photo ops to help the victims of the storm, whose sufferings have been neglected to this day. Having abdicated their most fundamental duty to "promote the general welfare," Bush's people (and their comrades in the right-wing media) focused not on how to help their stricken fellow-citizens but worked instead—as usual—to shift the blame. All their energy went into rapping Mayor Ray Nagin, Gov. Kathleen Blanco, and other, lesser state and city officers already battered by conditions so horrendous that even Venezuela, Cuba, and Honduras offered help (which the administration turned down). More than any other single event, the drowning of New Orleans defined Bush to the nation, and the world, with his blithe salute to

2005

1/4/05	1/24/05	2/25/05	3/20–21/05	3/31/05	7/1/05	7/7/05	8/1/05
Bush intends to reduce Social Security benefits by one-third over the next few decades, *The Washington Post* reports.	AARP comes out against Bush's plan to privatize Social Security.	A Florida judge rules that Terri Schiavo's feeding tube must be removed on March 18.	Congress passes, and Bush signs, emergency legislation to prevent removal of Schiavo's feeding tube.	The Supreme Court having once again refused her parents' case, Terri Schiavo dies.	Supreme Court Justice Sandra Day O'Connor announces her retirement.	*New York Times* reporter Judith Miller goes to prison for refusing to name a source who had talked to her about Valerie Plame's employment by the CIA.	Bush appoints John Bolton as U.S. ambassador to the United Nations.

FEMA's cabbage-brained director—"Brownie, you're doing a heck of a job!"—instantly becoming just as infamous a line as "Mission Accomplished."

From there Bush just kept lurching from one outrage to another throughout the dark remainder of the year. There was his effort to medievalize the Supreme Court—probably his most enduring legacy. The easy confirmation of far-right Republican John Roberts as Supreme Court Chief Justice, after William Rehnquist's sudden passing in September, was quickly followed by the president's abortive struggle to replace retiring Justice Sandra Day O'Connor with the wondrously unqualified Harriet Miers, White House Counsel and longtime Bush ultra-loyalist—a novel effort to appoint a footstool to the federal bench. That move having enraged his theocratic base, Bush rapidly atoned for it by naming, in her place, another far-right Republican, Samuel Alito. (See Dan Wasserman and David Horsey's views on pp. 226 and 231.)

In November, it emerged that Bush's new Attorney General, Alberto Gonzales, had eagerly (and secretly) obliged the administration's wish to be allowed to torture anyone they wanted in the "war on terror."

And in December, *The Washington Post*'s Dana Priest reported that the CIA had been carrying out "extreme renditions" of suspected terrorists to countries where official torture is routine. Finally, it came out in December that the federal government had been conducting mass surveillance of Americans without securing warrants—as if all of us were the "terrorists" that Bush and Cheney were ostensibly pursuing. (See Walt Handelsman's cartoon on p. 235.)

Bush's first year as a lame duck wrapped up with a staggering array of "accomplishments": a Supreme Court now hanging off the deep end, a White House pushing for the right to spy on all and torture anyone they wished, a major U.S. city devastated, a bloody war of occupation moving into its third year, and the country's international reputation sinking to new lows. But, for all that, the president's morale was still sky-high, and his "resolve" unshakable—a situation captured nicely in Wasserman's cartoon on p. 234, in which a buoyant Bush leafs happily through an issue of the *Baghdad Bugle* with the demented headline, "Everything's Fine!"

8/28/05	8/29/05	9/2/05	9/3/05	9/29/05	10/3/05	12/16/05
Katrina upgraded to a Category 5 hurricane. New Orleans evacuated. Bush warned of levee failure by Max Hastings, director of the National Hurricane Center.	Katrina makes landfall; levees in New Orleans give way. On the road promoting his Medicare plan, Bush does not respond to Louisiana Gov. Blanco's plea for assistance.	"Brownie, you're doing a heck of a job!"	Chief Justice of the Supreme Court William Rehnquist dies.	By a vote of 78–22, Senate confirms John Roberts as Chief Justice of the Supreme Court.	Bush nominates Harriet Miers as Supreme Court Justice.	*The New York Times* reports that, in 2002, Bush secretly authorized the NSA to monitor the telephone calls of U.S. citizens.

"And there is a new history now that has been done, and that history needs to be included in the process."

George W. Bush,
Bratislava, Slovakia, 2/24/05

In January, Bush began his campaign for tort reform, claiming that "frivolous litigation" was driving up health care costs. Sen. Edward Kennedy (D-Mass.) called Bush's plan "a shameful shield for drug companies and HMOs who hurt people through negligence."

"We look forward to analyzing and working with legislation that will make—it would hope—put a free press's mind at ease that you're not being denied information you shouldn't see."

George W. Bush,
Washington, D.C., 4/14/05

"We look forward to spreading freedom around the world."

George W. Bush,
Washington, D.C., 1/26/05

"In this job you've got a lot on your plate on a regular basis; you don't have much time to sit around and wander, lonely, in the Oval Office, kind of asking different portraits, 'How do you think my standing will be?'"

George W. Bush,
Washington, D.C., 3/16/05

"After all, Europe is America's closest ally."

George W. Bush,
Mainz, Germany, 2/23/05

After years of effort, on March 26 Republicans won a narrow Senate vote to open 1.5 million acres of once-protected Alaskan wilderness to oil exploration. Bush called the move a critical part of the nation's energy strategy.

"One of the great sources of energy for the future is liquefied natural gas. There's a lot of gas reserves around the world. Gas is—can only be transported by ship, though, when you liquefy it, when you put it in a solid form."

George W. Bush,
Washington, D.C., 4/28/05

GEORGE W. BUSH

"You're asking me whether or not people ought to be exposed to different ideas, the answer is yes."

George W. Bush, on whether intelligent design should be taught in schools, Washington, D.C., 8/1/05

In May, it was reported that the U.S. Air Force was seeking Bush's approval for a plan to develop and deploy precision weaponry in space. According to *The Guardian*, "The new weapons being studied range from hunter-killer satellites to orbiting weapons using lasers, radio waves, or even dense metal tubes dropped from space by a weapon known as 'Rods from God.'"

"'We haven't reached the point of strafing and bombing from space,' Pete Teets, who stepped down last month as the acting secretary of the air force, told a space-warfare symposium last year. 'Nonetheless, we are thinking about these possibilities.'"

New York Times, 5/18/05

"IN OUR POLLING NEARLY 60% OF THE PUBLIC SUPPORTS THE PATRIOT ACT. IT DROPS AROUND 35% WHEN WE TELL THEM WHAT IT ACTUALLY DOES."

"We discussed the way forward in Iraq, discussed the importance of a democracy in the greater Middle East in order to leave behind a peaceful tomorrow."

George W. Bush,
Tbilisi, Georgia, 5/10/05

In May, the *Times of London* published the so-called "Downing Street Memo," top-secret British intelligence documents from July 2002 that advised Tony Blair that the White House had "fixed" intelligence on Iraq and had been pushing for any excuse to invade. Rep. John Conyers (D-Mich.) said that the documents "establish a prima facie case of going to war under false pretenses."

"Well, we've made the decision to defeat the terrorists abroad so we don't have to face them here at home. And when you engage the terrorists abroad, it causes activity and action."

George W. Bush,
Washington, D.C., 4/28/05

"But Iraq has—have got people there that are willing to kill, and they're hard-nosed killers. And we will work with the Iraqis to secure their future."

George W. Bush,
Washington, D.C., 4/28/05

In July, a New York woman filed a federal discrimination lawsuit alleging she was forced to resign her Long Island elementary school teaching post by the principal who disliked her Republican activism and ordered her to remove a portrait of Bush from her classroom.

"THE THIN COATING OF SLIME MAKES IT EASIER TO SLIDE HIM UNDER THE DOOR."

On August 1, saying the job was "too important to leave vacant any longer, especially during a war and a vital debate about U.N. reform," Bush named the controversial (and legendarily combative) John Bolton as United Nations ambassador through a recess appointment, avoiding a likely contentious Senate nomination process.

SLOGAN
SLOGAN·ANOTHER SLOGAN·SLOGAN·NEW SLOGAN·SLOGAN
SLOGAN·SLOGAN·SLOGAN·SLOGAN·SLOGAN·SLOGAN
SLOGAN·SLOGAN·SLOGAN·ANOTHER NEW SLOGAN·SLOGAN
SLOGAN·SLOGAN
SLOGAN·SLOGAN
SLOGAN·SLOGAN
REVISED SLOGAN·SLOGAN

IRAQ EXIT STRATEGY

"See, in my line of work you got to keep repeating things over and over and over again for the truth to sink in, to kind of catapult the propaganda."

George W. Bush,
Greece, NY, 5/24/05

"MR. PRESIDENT, YOU SHOULD STAY AWAY FROM THIS SECTOR OF THE RANCH."

WHY?! ARE THERE TERRORISTS?!

"NO, JUST ANOTHER DEAD SOLDIER'S MOTHER WANTING TO ASK YOU SOME QUESTIONS."

"You see, not only did the attacks help accelerate a recession, the attacks reminded us that we are at war."

George W. Bush
on 9/11, Washington, D.C., 6/8/05

The Boy in the Bubble...

"It's a myth to think I don't know what's going on. It's a myth to think that I'm not aware that there's opinions that don't agree with mine, because I'm fully aware of that."

George W. Bush,
Philadelphia, 12/12/05

"And Brownie, you're doing a heck of a job."

George W. Bush, referring to the FEMA director's response to the Katrina disaster, Mobile, Ala., 9/2/05

"Out of the rubbles of Trent Lott's house—he's lost his entire house—there's going to be a fantastic house. And I'm looking forward to sitting on the porch."

George W. Bush, Mobile, Ala., 9/2/05

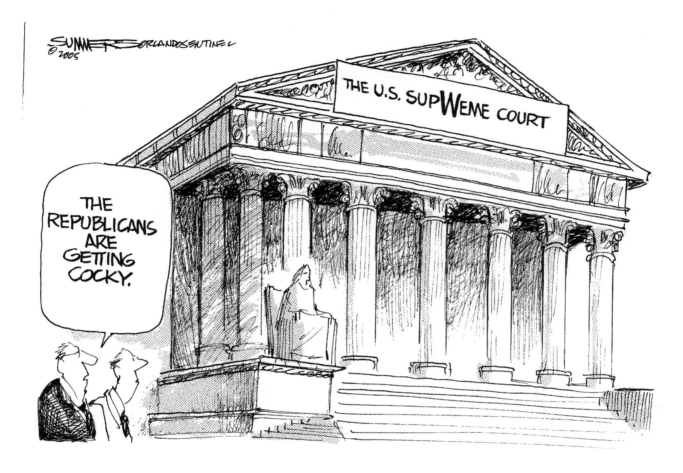

"The list is wide open, which should create some good speculation here in Washington. And make sure you notice when I said that I looked right at Al Gonzales, who can really create speculation."

George W. Bush on nominating a new
Supreme Court justice, Washington, D.C., 9/6/05

GULF COAST CLEANUP.

"My thoughts are, we're going to get somebody who knows what they're talking about when it comes to rebuilding cities."

George W. Bush,
Biloxi, Miss., 9/2/05

With the promise of lucrative post-Katrina reconstruction contracts from the government, Halliburton shares rose over 10 percent in early September.

VICE PRESIDENT CHENEY RECUPERATING AT HOME FROM DOUBLE KNEE SURGERY

> "I also reminded them that I think it's important to bring somebody from outside the system, the judicial system, somebody that hasn't been on the bench and, therefore, there's not a lot of opinions for people to look at."
>
> George W. Bush on nominating Harriet Miers for the Supreme Court, Washington, D.C., 10/4/05

"I think we are welcomed. But it was not a peaceful welcome."

George W. Bush,
Philadelphia, 12/12/05

In early October, Bush's approval rating hit a new low: 37 percent.

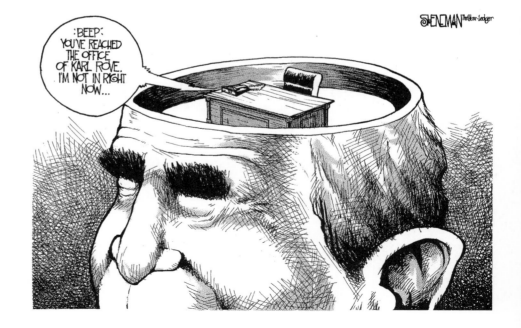

A poll taken in late September showed that 59 percent of Americans considered the invasion of Iraq a mistake.

♪ "ROVE-ROVE-ROVE" YOUR BOAT ♪

"The best place for the facts to be done is by somebody who's spent time investigating it."

George W. Bush, on the Plamegate affair,
Washington, D.C., 7/18/05

"We do not torture."

George W. Bush,
Panama City, 11/7/05

"We will lead the 21st century into a shining age of human liberty."

George W. Bush,
Washington, D.C., 9/11/05

"I mean, I read the newspaper. I mean, I can tell you what the headlines are. I must confess, if I think the story is, like, not a fair appraisal, I'll move on. But I know what the story's about."

George W. Bush,
Philadelphia, 12/12/05

"[I'm] occasionally reading, I want you to know, in the second term."

George W. Bush,
Washington, D.C., 3/16/05

A Kick in the Pants

By 2006, most Americans could see, or sense, that George W. Bush was an extraordinary president. If any other Chief Executive had kick-started a disastrous war *and* lost a major U.S. city to a storm that the whole country could see coming, he would then, at least, bend over backwards to appease the public, and thereby try to help his party climb out of the pit that he'd dug for them. Heading toward midterm elections, he might make a few big unexpected gestures to disarm his critics and woo back some disaffected voters—as, say, Nixon did in 1970, when he sought to stifle opposition to the Vietnam War by pushing Earth Day and other green initiatives.

Bush did nothing of the kind; he spent 2006 as if still posing for the cameras on that aircraft carrier. Katrina might as well have happened on another planet. Although, in mid-September 2005, he had grandly claimed "responsibility" for his government's astounding non-response to that disaster, over the next year he continued to do nothing for its thousands of impoverished victims (see Chan Lowe's cartoon of Bush's empty promises regarding New Orleans, p. 259). Instead, the administration diligently worked to gentrify the region, a plan that paid off politically: all those Democratic voters were dispersed to parts unknown, or stuck in out-of-state internment camps where no accommodations were made for casting ballots in New Orleans's mayoral elections in the spring. When Bush did mention Katrina, his tongue betrayed his unconcern: "I'm a strong proponent of the restoration of the wetlands," he said in March. "The stronger the wetlands, the more likely the damage of the hurricane."

Bush was just as blithe about the war. As Iraq slid ever deeper into chaos, with the number of American dead surpassing the official 9/11 toll, Bush kept noting unnamed "signs of progress" through mid-August (on May 1 he had discerned a "turning point"). He also then argued that, bad as things looked now and then—"Sometimes I'm frustrated," he conceded—they could be a whole lot worse. Certainly he would *not* fire Secretary of Defense Donald Rumsfeld, whom, before Election Day, he kept on hailing despite the latter's criminal incompetence, his horrifying facetiousness, a callous jokiness that rivaled Bush's own, and the fact that he was openly detested by many soldiers and officers alike.

Nor was it only on the subjects of Iraq and New Orleans that Bush flouted public sentiment. On issue after issue, from stem cell research to immigration to the Supreme Court (Samuel Alito was confirmed in early January with just four Democratic Senate votes—seven more than the far less accomplished Clarence Thomas had received in 1991), Bush continued to make clear that he just *didn't care* what We the People think.

Surely some of that bizarre indifference is a symptom of the president's messiah complex: his firm belief that "God speaks through me," as he said in Pennsylvania on July 16, 2004, and his inability to name a single thing that, if he had the chance, he would do differently today. And yet psychology alone cannot explain Bush's overt contempt for mass opinion; for that contempt is clearly shared by Cheney, Rove, and others near the president, yet they don't have (as far as we know) long chats with Jesus. Rather, their extraordinary disregard for popular opinion is squarely based on their control of the election system, which they have largely rigged through the e-voting machinery (now used by over 80 percent of the electorate), and a partisan corps of U.S. Attorneys.

Such electoral certainty no doubt explains why Bush & Co. remained unfazed throughout the countdown to Election Day, even as congressional Republicans were jumping ship and Democratic candidates were giggling up their sleeves. (Three weeks before the vote, Bush and Rove struck "even their closest allies as almost inexplicably upbeat," according to *The Washington Post*.) Whereas Bill Clinton had repented (often) to defuse his scandals, whether they were based on something real (his trysts with Monica Lewinsky) or not (the flap over his haircut on *Air Force One*, which had allegedly delayed flights at LAX), this White House stayed strangely cool regardless of all sorts of huge embarrassments: when Cheney shot his hunting buddy in the face in February (a stroke of recklessness that Matt Davies, on p. 245, pithily compares to Cheney's quest for those Iraqi WMDs), or when Bush spooked German chancellor Angela Merkel with an impromptu public backrub in July. As Election Day approached, and Republican candidates were all but asking Bush to stay the hell away from them in public, the regime's cocksureness was undiminished even by such setbacks as the CIA's finding, reported in late September, that "the Iraq war has spawned a new generation of terrorists," or the news, in early October, of North Korea's first nuclear test.

Atypically, the media played up such stories, and, in those decisive last weeks, also took some other, harder shots at the Bush White House: a rare assault suggesting that the GOP's congressional incumbents were not the only ones alarmed by Bush's recklessness. In late September, ABC News broke the story of Rep. Mark Foley's hanky-panky with young (male) congressional pages, and the corporate media piled on. That imbroglio, which swiftly led to Foley's resignation, was something new in recent U.S. politics: a good old-fashioned sex scandal involving not a Democrat but a holier-than-thou Republican. Then, on October 2, Bob Woodward came out with *State of Denial*, the explosive—and incongruous—third volume in his trilogy *Bush at War*. Whereas the first two books were classics of post-9/11 hero worship, this one was a searing (if belated) exposé of the administration's bogus buildup to the occupation of Iraq. The media duly magnified the book's most damning revelations (and the cartoonists had a field day with it, as in Drew Sheneman's and Taylor Jones's works on pp. 267 and 271).

That late blast of troubling news hurt the Republicans—so did the tremendous national turnout on Election Day. At 41.3 percent, it was officially the highest off-year turnout since 1970. Just as in 2004, though, the elections in 2006 were broadly marked by electronic voting machine shortages and breakdowns, widespread ballot "spoilage," blunt intimidation tactics, campaigns of disinformation, and a host of other antidemocratic tricks and seeming accidents— nearly all of which advantaged the Republicans. Throughout the country, once again, numerous pro-Bush incumbents eked out startling victories that defied the pre-election polls. Five Democrats—four of them in Florida—contested their "defeats," and elsewhere citizens demanded recounts or investigations.

Such hue and cry at the grass roots did not compel the Democratic Party's leadership to look into the problems on Election Day. Thrilled at having reclaimed both the House and Senate, the punch-drunk Democrats did not dare make an issue of the races they should have won. Thus, despite their partial

	1/31/06	2/11/06	4/4/06	4/29/06	5/11/06	7/11/06	7/17/06	8/3/06
2006	By a vote of 58–42, the Senate confirms Samuel Alito as an Associate Justice of the Supreme Court.	On a quail hunt at a friend's south Texas ranch, Cheney accidentally shoots Texas lawyer Harry Whittington, 78, in the face and neck.	Saddam Hussein formally charged with genocide at his trial in Iraq.	Stephen Colbert skewers Bush (and the media) at the annual awards dinner of the White House Correspondents Association.	Bush has a 29 percent approval rating, the lowest of his presidency, according to a Harris poll.	The U.S. Army discontinues a multibillion-dollar Halliburton contract, after audits find over $1 billion in questionable charges by the company.	At the G8 Summit in St. Petersburg, Bush surprises German chancellor Angela Merkel with an impromptu public backrub.	Iraq is on the brink of civil war, CENTCOM commander Gen. John Abizaid tells a Senate panel.

sweep, they failed to act as boldly as their mandate would allow, and at yet another moment of grave danger to the nation.

With the passage of the Military Commissions Act of 2006 on October 17, Bush repealed the right to *habeas corpus* for resident aliens and foreign nationals. Meanwhile, his war dragged hideously on, the toll on all sides climbing exponentially—as many as 655,000 Iraqis had by now been killed, reported the medical journal *The Lancet* on October 1—and the situation likely to get even grimmer after the barbaric hanging of Saddam Hussein on December 29. Earlier in December, Bush's dismissal of the Baker-Hamilton Report's call for a gradual drawdown of U.S. troop strength in Iraq caused loud dismay throughout official Washington—as if Bush had not *always* shrugged off arguments that he just didn't want to hear, however cogent they might be. (Jones, Jack Ohman, and Davies noted the obtuseness of the president's response, on pp. 269, 270, and 272.) As 2006 drew to a close, it was more obvious than ever that this nation was confronting unprecedented dangers. As Lowe trenchantly suggests in his cartoon on p. 268, it was the president *himself* who now appeared to pose the very threat that he and his regime had always warned against.

9/28/06	9/30/06	10/17/06	11/1/06	11/7/06	11/8/06	12/6/06	12/29/06
ABC News publishes salacious e-mails between Rep. Mark Foley and a congressional page. Foley resigns the next day.	Publication of Bob Woodward's *State of Denial: Bush at War, Part III*.	Bush signs the Military Commissions Act, effectively repealing *habeas corpus*.	Resignation of Ted Haggard as director of the National Association of Evangelicals, after news breaks of his relations with gay prostitute Mike Jones.	Election Day. Republicans lose control of both the House and Senate.	Donald Rumsfeld resigns as Secretary of Defense, replaced by Robert Gates.	Iraq study group report released, recommending speedy withdrawal of troops and expanded diplomatic relations with Iraq's neighbors.	Saddam Hussein hanged.

"There is an enemy out there. They read newspapers."

George W. Bush criticizing media exposure of
his secret domestic surveillance program,
Fort Sam Houston, Texas, 1/1/06

"I AM THE PRESIDENT. I DON'T NEED WARRANTS."

TRIBUNE MEDIA SERVICE
WWW.CONRADPROJECTS.COM

"Yes, I said it's possible that they would have met at a holiday reception or some other widely attended gathering. The President does not know [Jack Abramoff], nor does the President recall ever meeting him."

White House press secretary
Scott McClellan, Washington, D.C., 1/4/06

WHITE HOUSE RELEASES
BUSH/ABRAMOFF PHOTOS

To help folks understand the president's State of the Union address, here's a handy **Glossary of Terms...**

"OWNERSHIP SOCIETY"
(IF YOU'RE POOR, YOU'RE ON YOUR OWN.)

"PERMANENT TAX CUTS"
(PERMANENT DEFICITS FOR AMERICA.)

"PLAN FOR VICTORY"
(WE'RE GONNA BE IN IRAQ A LONG, LONG TIME.)

"SPENDING RESTRAINTS"
(BILLIONS FOR IRAQ, CUTS FOR FOOD STAMPS.)

"TERRORIST SURVEILLANCE"
(SPY ON ANYONE, ANYWHERE, ANYTIME.)

"VISIONARY AGENDA"
(BEAT THE DEMOCRATS IN NOVEMBER.)

©2006
SEATTLE POST-
INTELLIGENCER
TRIBUNE MEDIA SERVICES
HORSEY

"Now, we've had idiots as presidents before. He's not unique. But he's certainly the most active idiot that we have ever had."

Gore Vidal, responding to Bush's
State of the Union address, 1/31/06

{ Prior to Bush's State of the Union address, antiwar activist Cindy Sheehan was arrested in the House of Representatives gallery for refusing to cover up a T-shirt reading, "2,245 Dead. How many more?"

"Well, you can't anticipate everything."

Dick Cheney on the Iraq insurgency,
NewsHour with Jim Lehrer, 2/7/06

"I like my buddies from West Texas. I liked them when I was young, I liked them then I was middle-age, I liked them before I was President, and I like them during President and I like them after President."

George W. Bush,
Nashville, 2/1/06

"It's a necessary agreement. It's one that will help both our peoples."

George W. Bush on the signing of a historic nuclear technology deal with India, New Delhi, 3/2/06

"Out of thousands and thousands of admirals and generals, if every time two or three people disagreed, we changed the secretary of defense of the United States, it would be like a merry-go-round."

Secretary of Defense Donald Rumsfeld, responding to the numerous generals calling for his resignation, 4/7/06

On April 14, *Bloomberg News* reported that Dick and Lynn Cheney's total income in 2005 was $8,824,762, mostly from stock options Cheney received before stepping down as chairman of Halliburton, "the world's largest oilfield-services company," before the 2000 campaign.

PRESIDENTS BUSH AND HU DISCUSS HUMAN RIGHTS

"Do you want this job, Snow? Do you want to face these pinheads, these unbelievable cretins in the White House briefing room every day? Why do you want to do that?"

Bill O'Reilly, interviewing Tony Snow about rumors he was to be named the new White House press secretary, 4/21/06

> "Bush's confidence goes well beyond comfort in his own skin. He exhibits a sincere, passionate, and uncompromising conviction in his principles. . . . It's that kind of certainty that drives Bush's critics batty."
>
> Rich Lowry, *National Review Online*, 9/13/06

"I'm the decider, and I decide what is best."

George W. Bush,
Washington, D.C., 4/18/06

"You never know what your history is going to be like until long after you're gone."

George W. Bush,
Washington, D.C., 5/5/06

"SEE IF YOU CAN GET BRAD AND ANGELINA TO HAVE ANOTHER BABY. THE PRESS IS STARTING TO COVER REAL NEWS AGAIN."

"*The New York Times* and other news organizations ought to think long and hard about whether a public's right to know in some cases might override somebody's right to live."

Tony Snow,
Washington, D.C., 6/26/06

"We shouldn't fear a world that is more interacted."

George W. Bush,
Washington, D.C., 6/27/06

THE PRESIDENT FINALLY ADDRESSES THE NAACP

SHENEMAN TheStar-Ledger

"THE REPUBLICAN PARTY HAS WRITTEN OFF THE AFRICAN-AMERICAN VOTE FOR TOO LONG, AND NOW THAT WHITE PEOPLE DON'T LIKE US, IT'S TIME FOR THAT TO CHANGE."

Writing about Bush's uneasy reception when he addressed the NAACP convention on July 20, the *Washington Post*'s Dana Milbank noted, "The booing, like the heckling, was omitted from the White House transcript."

A year after Katrina, the federal government's response was widely viewed as slow and ineffective. The Government Accountability Office concluded in June that FEMA wasted between $600 million and $1.4 billion alone on "improper and potentially fraudulent individual assistance payments."

"This shows the president is more interested in science fiction than science."

Clean Air Watch president Frank O'Donnell, on learning of Bush's favorable 2004 meeting with global warming denier and author Michael Crichton, 2/19/06

TONY BLAIR

"It should have been very obvious to us."

Tony Blair, on underestimating
the strength of the Iraqi insurgency,
Washington, D.C., 5/25/06

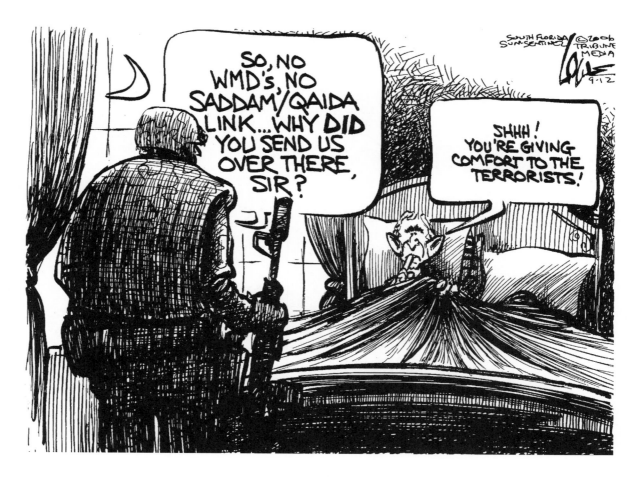

"As you can probably see I was injured myself, not here at the hospital but in combat with a cedar. I eventually won."

George W. Bush,
Brooke Army Medical Center,
San Antonio, Texas, 1/1/06

In May, Amnesty International compared Bush's tactics for fighting terrorism—particularly his alleged acceptance of torture and careless disregard for civil liberties—to those utilized in Augusto Pinochet's Chile and Hafez Assad's Syria.

"You know, one of the hardest parts of my job is to connect Iraq to the war on terror."

George W. Bush,
Washington, D.C., 9/6/06

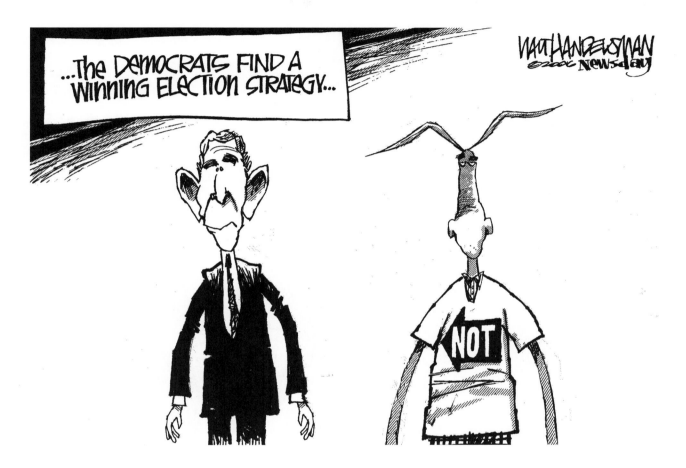

"You know, when I campaigned here in 2000, I said, I want to be a war President. No President wants to be a war President, but I am one."

George W. Bush,
Des Moines, 10/26/06

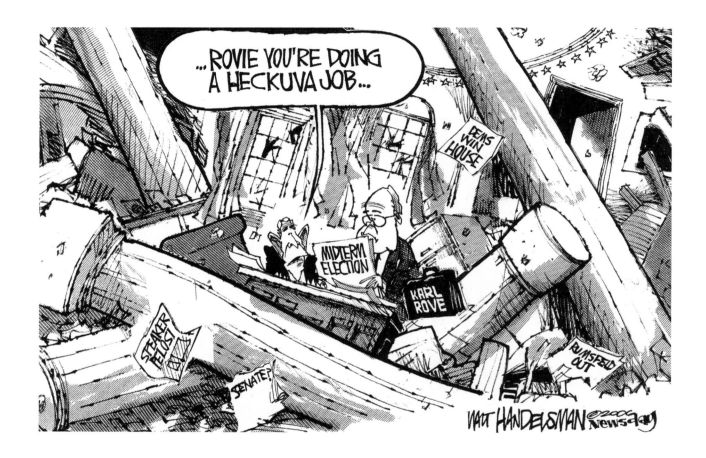

In the 2006 midterm election, Democrats retook control of both the House and Senate for the first time since 1994. On November 8 Bush said, "I'm obviously disappointed with the outcome of the election and, as the head of the Republican Party, I share a large part of the responsibility."

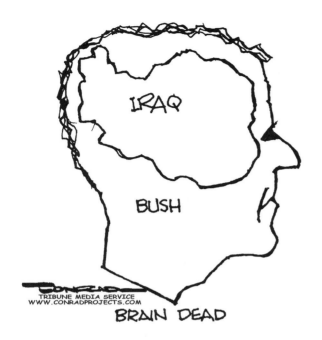

IRAQ

BUSH

TRIBUNE MEDIA SERVICE
WWW.CONRADPROJECTS.COM

BRAIN DEAD

"This business about graceful exit [from Iraq] just simply has no realism to it at all."

George W. Bush,
Amman, Jordan, 11/30/06

"YOU COME UP WITH A COHERENT IRAQ POLICY, THEN YOU CAN SIT AT THE ADULT TABLE."

HOW WOULD HOMELAND SECURITY RANK *THIS* TRAVELER?

©2006
TRIBUNE MEDIA
12-2
SOUTH FLORIDA
SUN-SENTINEL

- DIFFICULTY WITH THE ENGLISH LANGUAGE

- DOES NOT CHECK ANY BAGGAGE

- CONTROLS WEAPONS OF MASS DESTRUCTION

- HOLDS EXTREMIST POSITIONS

- NEVER BUYS ROUND-TRIP TICKETS

- HAS HISTORY OF INSTIGATING VIOLENT CONFLICTS

{ An international public opinion survey revealed in November that a majority of people in Britain, Canada, and Mexico considered Bush a threat to world peace, ranking closely with North Korea's Kim Jong-il and Iran's Mahmoud Ahmadinejad.

"And the question is, are we going to be facile enough to change with— will we be nimble enough; will we be able to deal with the circumstances on the ground? And the answer is, yes, we will."

George W. Bush,
Washington, D.C., 7/25/06

THIS MUST BE THE ADMINISTRATION'S HORRIFYINGLY BUNGLED IRAQ QUAGMIRE!

NO. THIS IS THE ADMINISTRATION'S HORRIFYINGLY BUNGLED FEMA QUAGMIRE!

GEORGE W. BUSH

"And truth of the matter is, a lot of reports in Washington are never read by anybody. To show you how important this one is, I read it, and our guest read it."

George W. Bush, speaking with Blair about the
Baker-Hamilton Report, Washington, D.C., 12/7/06

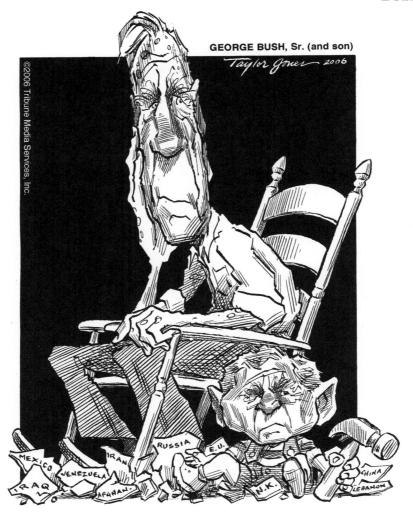

GEORGE BUSH, Sr. (and son)

"In the event that Baker actually advocates [in the Iraq Study Group report] what he thinks, Bush's options will be to admit the errors of his ways and the wisdom of his father and father's men or to cast them and caution aside once again. His choice is either Shakespearean or Wagnerian."

Sidney Blumenthal, *Salon.com*, 11/16/06

"Today I heard from some opinions that matter a lot to me, and these are the opinions of those who wear the uniform."

George W. Bush,
on "the way forward" in Iraq,
Washington, D.C., 12/13/06

"Because of your work, children who once wanted to die are now preparing to live."

George W. Bush
at a White House summit on malaria,
Washington, D.C., 12/14/06

No Tree Left Behind

On January 3, with the start of the 110th United States Congress—Democratic-controlled for the first time since 1994—it seemed that we might finally see dramatic change. For six years we had watched the same intolerable spectacle of high crimes paying off handsomely for Bush et al, with every hint of some comeuppance fizzing out. But now, at long last, it seemed that Bush had been rebuked in no uncertain terms—his party got "a thumpin'," as he himself had quaintly put it—and so help was on the way. For all his sunny talk of compromise, Bush continued to respect the other party, and the voters, about as much as he had prior to Election Day; and so he seemed to look right through "the Democrat majority," as he invidiously put it in his State of the Union speech on January 23.

That speech was itself a fine example of the administration's cynical contempt for its opponents and the citizens who had elected them (Walt Handelsman's cartoon on p. 292 points to some of what Bush *didn't* mention in his speech). Bush devoted several verdant paragraphs to "America's energy supply," culminating in a challenge to "reduce gasoline usage in the United States by 20 percent in the next ten years" (loud applause).

This "great goal," he said, would mean producing new supplies of ethanol, "using everything from wood chips to grasses to agricultural wastes." It would also mean relying more on "solar and wind energy," "plug-in and hybrid vehicles," "clean diesel vehicles and biodiesel fuel." Such technologies "will enable us to live our lives less dependent on oil," the oilman said—and, he added grandly, "they will help us to confront the serious challenge of global climate change" (loud applause).

Of course, that faux-green passage was pure Astro-Turf. Any half-attentive listener would have noticed that those eco-friendly phrases were mixed smoothly with such toxic references as "greater use of clean coal technology" and "clean, safe nuclear power." It took a colossal disrespect for the intelligence of his audience for Bush to think that they would hear some pastoral promise in his declaration that "we must step up domestic oil production in environmentally sensitive ways." In any case, the hollowness of that performance became apparent in the next few months, as Bush proposed to sell off some 300,000 acres of our national forests, rejected the Kyoto Protocol (again), and tried to gut the Endangered Species Act. Most brazenly, Bush's EPA attempted to avoid enforcing the Clean Air Act, although even the right-dominated Supreme Court ruled, on April 2, that the agency could not ignore the law, no matter how much Bush and Cheney might want it to.

While that crime has gone largely unreported, the press did play up other scandals, which Bush then handled in his usual way. On February 18, *The Washington Post* reported on the vile conditions inside Building 18 at Walter Reed Army Medical Center, where wounded troops had been left to rot in shocking squalor. As he did after Katrina (although more quickly and apologetically), Bush responded with a photo op, visiting the patients at the place and promising to clean it up; and several heads soon rolled. That show of fatherly concern would probably have been more credible, and surely would have done more good, if it had happened two years earlier, when UPI's Mark Benjamin first exposed the harrowing plight of "the invisible wounded" at Walter Reed.

Bush dealt just as cynically with the resurgent scandal over his warrantless surveillance program here at home. On January 4, it was reported that, in a "signing statement" of December 20, while Congress was in recess, Bush had claimed the right to read the private mail of U.S. citizens if there should be what he called an "emergency." Two weeks later, the White House appeared to backtrack by announcing that its controversial telephone surveillance program, managed by the NSA, would henceforth be accountable to the Foreign Intelligence Surveillance Court, which would pre-approve all wiretaps *in that program*. Then, in early March, Mark Klein, a whistle-blower at AT&T, revealed that the NSA was operating "secret rooms" inside the company's switching centers in several cities. Such collaboration allows the agency—ostensibly committed to monitoring only *overseas* communications—to suck up an oceanic flood of private information. It was "an illegal and Orwellian project," as Klein remarked, and yet the revelation bounced right off the presidential juggernaut.

But the biggest scandal was yet to come—an outrage so immense that it made even Plamegate look like small potatoes. (That case seemed to climax on March 6, when Lewis "Scooter" Libby, Cheney's former chief of staff and Bush's patsy, was convicted on four counts of lying and obstruction of justice; his 30-month sentence was commuted by Bush on July 2.) In January, it came out that the White House, working closely with Attorney General Alberto Gonzales, had purged the U.S. Department of Justice, forcing out attorneys who had not put the party first, replacing them with dirty tricksters, opposition researchers, and theocratic activists. (The purge of Justice recalled Bush's drive to staff the Iraq occupation with true believers only, regardless of ability, if any.) The Gonzales scandal broke after the summary dismissal, in late 2006, of eight U.S. Attorneys: ostensibly for "poor performance," but actually for failing, or refusing, to serve Bush's political agenda by investigating bogus claims of Democratic "voter fraud." In other words, the scandal shed some light not only on the party's fight to snatch up bureaucratic turf, but on their long crusade to block the vote.

As ever, Bush waved off the crisis as a big impertinence, asserting his rock-hard support for the Attorney General, whose long flights of amnesiac testimony, both in Congress and before the press, embarrassed everyone except himself (and Bush). Gonzales's "forgetfulness" became still more embarrassing when his own late confederates took the stand and contradicted him. Yet Bush still regally defended his old crony, telling Congress they should wrap it up, and "get on [with] the business of passing legislation."

Thus Bush kept right on partying as if it were 2002, regardless of his party's "thumpin'" in the last election. Blowing off the Iraq Study Group, which called for a new strategy to lay the groundwork for eventual withdrawal, in January Bush announced a "surge" of roughly 21,000 more troops to hold Baghdad. The plan did not impress the war's supporters. Initially the Pentagon had estimated that the occupation would require *half a million* troops (not the 150,000 that Sec. Rumsfeld had deemed sufficient). It was therefore hard to see what five brigades could do, said those who wanted "more boots on the ground." Nor did the "surge" appeal to critics of the war, who, along with most Americans, called for U.S. disengagement, whether slow or swift, and not a halfway measure that would just prolong the agony. (Chan Lowe and Matt Davies captured the unpopularity of Bush's plan, on pp. 282 and 283.) Lost in all such clamor was the disconcerting fact that Bush's "surge" was actually much larger than he claimed. On February 1, the Congressional Budget Office pointed out that Bush's reckoning had not included the support troops who would also have to go along—at least 15,000, bringing the grand total to about 35,000 more Americans sent to Iraq.

1/23/07	2/7/07	3/6/07	3/22/07	3/29/07	4/18/07	4/21/07
In his State of the Union address, Bush proposes ending U.S. dependence on foreign oil, and acknowledges the threat of global warming.	Court-martial of Army Lt. Ehren Watada, who had refused on legal grounds to serve in the Iraq war, ends in mistrial.	Lewis "Scooter" Libby convicted on four out of five charges in Plamegate case.	International Red Cross reports abuse of CIA detainees at Guantánamo.	Kyle Sampson, former chief of staff to Alberto Gonzales, testifies that Gonzales's account of the U.S. Attorney scandal is "inaccurate."	Supreme Court upholds ban on late-term abortions.	The National Association of Evangelicals deplores the government's use of torture in the "war on terror."

2007

Whatever its true size, and however hard Bush tried to package it as something new, his "surge" was just more of the same old no-win policy that the voters had rejected on Election Day. But it was not just his fault that the national narrative refused to budge, for Bush and his cohorts were not alone in acting like the last election hadn't happened. Throughout the first half of the year, the Democrats in Congress seemed to be afraid of taking charge. Although they quickly made great strides on certain narrow fronts, the Democrats collectively tiptoed around the regime's lawlessness, as deferential to this president as the House Republicans had been ferocious in attacking Clinton. It was the Democrats who took impeachment off the table, ignored the issue of election fraud, and, finally, voted to keep funding Bush's war on Bush's terms (a cave-in savaged by Chan Lowe on p. 308). It was not until the end of June that they finally started acting like an opposition party, stung into resistance by the endless war, the deepening U.S. Attorney scandal, and Dick Cheney's mad claim that Vice President is not part of the government's executive branch (see David Horsey's diagram of Cheney's argument, p. 318).

While the Democrats kept rowing Bush's boat, although they'd been elected to stand up to him, there was a major mutiny by those Republicans who had done the most to put him where he was, *despite* the voters. In May, the president's nativist minority exploded over his pro-business immigration bill; and he responded with the sort of shot that he *and* they had all been taking at the rest of us for years: Those who "want to kill the bill," he said, "don't want to do what's right for America." And so, with his approval ratings sinking even lower than Nixon's, Bush squared off against a livid army of his own crusaders—a major rift within the very movement that had crowned him in the first place.

America could not wait to get rid of him. Eighteen months before the next election, the field was crammed with both Republicans and Democrats competing for Bush's job, the former rarely mentioning his name, even as they largely parroted his most extreme positions. (At a GOP candidates' debate in May, three of the contenders boasted that they don't believe in evolution.) Thus Bush was "a uniter" after all, as all sides were largely unified against him. The national mood of bitter weariness was captured nicely in Dan Wasserman's cartoon (on p. 310) of the "Mission Accomplished" banner now in tatters, so that the only letters left spell out "I lied"; as one of Bush's men advises him, "After four years, it's showing some wear."

4/24/07	5/7/07	5/8/07	5/22/07	6/26/07	7/2/07
Rep. Dennis Kucinich (D-Ohio) introduces Articles of Impeachment against Dick Cheney.	Without examining the evidence, the House Administration Committee votes unanimously to dismiss the petitions of three Florida Democrats contesting their defeats in the 2006 election.	Queen Elizabeth visits the White House, where Bush winks at her and compares her to his mother.	Congressional Democrats approve war funding bill with no conditions for U.S. withdrawal.	The new-look Supreme Court hands down four decisions that portend difficult times ahead for the rights to free speech, separation of church and state, clean elections, and the environment.	Bush commutes Libby's two-and-a-half-year sentence, bringing instant praise from conservatives and denunciation from liberals.

In late December 2006, the Bush administration proposed listing the polar bear as an endangered species, implicitly acknowledging that the species is directly threatened by the effects of man-made global warming.

In March, an internal memo from the Fish and Wildlife Service was leaked that reminded U.S. scientists traveling abroad of "the administration's position on climate change, polar bears, and sea ice" and that they should avoid speaking about any of those issues.

"This is not a change in law, this is not new."

Tony Snow, on the December 20
presidential signing statement that granted
the federal government authority to open
domestic mail without warrants,
Washington, D.C., 1/5/07

> "A small, short surge would be the worst of all worlds."
>
> Sen. John McCain (R-Ariz.),
> remarks to the Senate
> Armed Services Committee
> backing Bush's plan,
> 1/12/07

A little over a month after the Iraq Study Group report called the situation in Iraq "grave and deteriorating," Bush announced a "surge" of more than 21,000 additional U.S. troops into Iraq to quell the spiraling violence.

As of January 31, 2007, at least 3,083 American service personnel had died in Iraq, with more than 23,000 wounded.

"The best way to defeat the totalitarian of hate is with an ideology of hope—an ideology of hate—excuse me—with an ideology of hope."

George W. Bush,
Fort Benning, Ga., 1/11/07

"The new strategy I outline tonight will change America's course in Iraq."

George W. Bush,
Washington, D.C., 1/10/07

"I've heard he's been called Bush's poodle. He's bigger than that."

George W. Bush,
discussing Tony Blair in
The Sun, 6/27/07

...PHASED WITHDRAWAL FROM REALITY...

"[Bush is] basically taking the nation into another nightmare of conflict over a war that no one sees any end to."

Iraq Study Group member Leon Panetta, quoted in *The New York Times*, 1/10/07

SIMPLE MULTIPLICATION

LADIES AND GENTLEMEN, THE NEXT PRESIDENT OF THE UNITED STATES.

"I am going to level with you, the president has said [the Iraq war] is going to be left to his successor. I think it is the height of irresponsibility and I really resent it."

Sen. Hillary Clinton (D-N.Y.),
Davenport, Iowa, 1/28/07

"I think if you look at what's transpired in Iraq, Chris, we have, in fact, made enormous progress."

Dick Cheney to Fox News's
Chris Wallace, 1/14/07

"The president's response to the challenge of Iraq is to send more American soldiers into the crossfire of the civil war that has engulfed that nation. . . Escalation of this war is not the change the American people called for in the last election."

Sen. Dick Durbin (D-Ill.), 1/10/07

"As far as the adverse impact on the nation around the world, this administration has been the worst in history."

Jimmy Carter,
Arkansas Democrat-Gazette, 5/19/07

"We will work with others to prevent Iran from gaining nuclear weapons and dominating the region."

George W. Bush,
Washington, D.C., 1/10/07

"And there is distrust in Washington. I am surprised, frankly, at the amount of distrust that exists in this town. And I'm sorry it's the case, and I'll work hard to try to elevate it."

George W. Bush,
National Public Radio, 1/29/07

"We need additional funds for transitioning to making more energy crops for our national security."

Sen. Tom Harkin (D-Iowa)
on Bush's corn-based
ethanol fuel plan, 1/22/07

Though touching on economy, education, healthcare, immigration, terrorism and Iraq, Bush said nothing about the massively difficult and ongoing reconstruction of New Orleans and the Gulf Coast in his State of the Union address.

"I think that the vice president is a person reflecting a half-glass-full mentality."

George W. Bush,
National Public Radio, 1/29/07

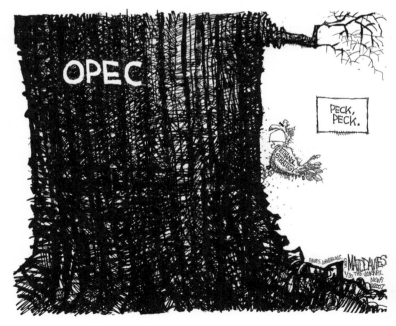

"KEEP AN EYE ON THIS CHAVEZ GUY. WITH ALL THAT POWER, HE'S LIABLE TO GO OFF AND DO SOMETHING STUPID."

In January, one of Bush's greatest regional critics, Venezuelan president Hugo Chavez (who famously called Bush "the devil" at the United Nations in September 2006), was given the power by the Congress to essentially bypass the legislature and rule by decree.

U.N. CALLS FOR GLOBAL WARMING SUMMIT...

"We know that the White House possesses documents that contain evidence of an attempt by senior administration officials to mislead the public by injecting doubt into the science of global warming and minimize the potential danger."

Rep. Henry Waxman (D-Calif.), 1/30/07

"And one thing we want during this war on terror is for people to feel like their life's moving on, that they're able to make a living and send their kids to college and put more money on the table."

George W. Bush,
NewsHour with Jim Lehrer, 1/16/07

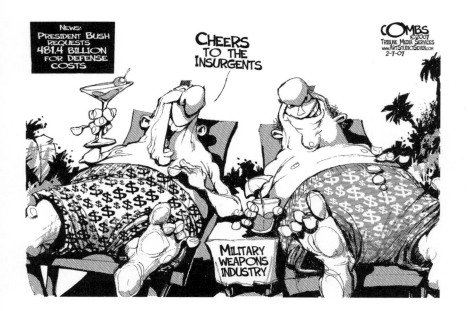

Bush's defense budget request of $481.4 billion was the biggest since the Reagan-era buildup of the 1980s. His requested $141.7 billion in supplemental funding for Iraq and Afghanistan pushed the cost in real terms for those conflicts past the total spent on the Vietnam War.

THE UNIMPEACHABLE

TRIBUNE MEDIA SERVICE
WWW.CONRADPROJECTS.COM

"Mr. President, we tried a monarchy once. It's not suited to America."

Sen. Chuck Hagel (R-Neb.), 3/28/07

"REMEMBER, DON'T MENTION NORTH KOREA. IF HE FINDS OUT WE SOLVED A CONFLICT DIPLOMATICALLY, HE'LL FREAK. IF HE ASKS, CHANGE THE SUBJECT OR TRY TO DISTRACT HIM WITH SOMETHING SHINY."

"To say that the United States has pursued diplomacy with North Korea is a little bit misleading."

Noam Chomsky, *AlterNet*, 2/26/07

"I think long-term when we look back on this period of time [the invasion of Iraq and death of Saddam Hussein] will be a remarkable achievement."

Dick Cheney,
The Weekend Australian, 2/23/07

"I wish the Iranian people well, and only hope their experience with an inept, rigid ideologue president goes better than ours."

Oliver Stone, on being called "[part of the] Great Satan" by Iranian President Mahmoud Ahmadinejad, Associated Press, 7/2/07,

I can't imagine a circumstance in which it's a good thing that [the U.S. military's] flexibility is constrained by people sitting here in Washington, sitting in the Congress trying to micromanage this war. It just—I don't think it's a good thing.

Secretary of State Condoleeza Rice,
Fox News Sunday, 2/25/07

"Some call this civil war; others call it emergency—I call it pure evil."

George W. Bush,
Washington, D.C., 3/28/07

In March, Democratic politicians began to call for an investigation into the firings of several U.S. attorneys during what they alleged was a partisan purge led by Attorney General Alberto Gonzales at the behest of the White House. Bush immediately opposed the attempt to subpoena White House staff.

WHITE HOUSE INTERVIEWING CANDIDATES TO REPLACE FIRED U.S. ATTORNEYS

"I also want to say something to the U.S. attorneys who resigned. I appreciate your service to the country."

George W. Bush, Washington, D.C., 3/20/07

W   GONZALES   ROVE

"To be sure, I have been—I should have been more precise when discussing this matter."

Alberto Gonzales,
discussing his actions in the firing of
eight U.S. attorneys, at the Senate
Judiciary Oversight Hearing, 4/19/07

"Under the clear terms of the Clean Air Act, EPA can avoid taking further action only if it determines that greenhouse gases do not contribute to climate change or if it provides some reasonable explanation."

Justice John Paul Stephens's majority Supreme Court decision in *Massachusetts v. EPA*, 4/2/07

"I KNOW ALL THE TALK FROM THE DEMOCRATS ABOUT SENDING YOU HOME WAS UNDERCUTTING MORALE. SO WE ADDED 3 MONTHS TO YOUR TOUR, JUST TO CHEER YOU UP."

"There are some similarities, of course [between Iraq and Vietnam] . . . Death is terrible."

George W. Bush,
Tipp City, Ohio, 4/19/07

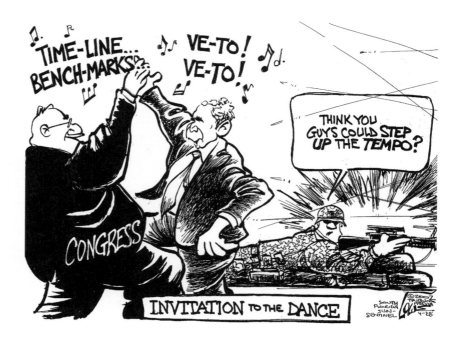

As of May 30, at least 3,467 American service personnel had died in Iraq since the invasion. In May alone, at least 90 Iraqi security personnel and 2,077 Iraqi civilians were killed.

"That's life in many ways. Um, I wish it were a just easy, straight line progression from birth to death but that's not the way it works."

George W. Bush,
ABC News, 4/18/07

"I could be."

George W. Bush, on whether he
was partly to blame for ending
Tony Blair's premiership,
Washington, D.C., 5/17/07

In May, John Ashcroft's former deputy John Comey testified to the Senate Judiciary Committee that on March 10, 2004, he raced to Ashcroft's hospital room in order to stop Alberto Gonzales and Andrew Card (respectively White House counsel and chief of staff, at the time) from trying to convince the extremely ill Ashcroft to reauthorize Bush's domestic eavesdropping program.

"The National Oceanic and Atmospheric Administration is spending up to $4 million to publicize a 200th anniversary celebration while the agency has cut $700,000 from hurricane research."

U.S. News & World Report, 5/17/07

"I wanted to congratulate [President Vladimir Putin] for being the only person that caught a fish. A fine catch."

George W. Bush,
Kennebunkport, Maine, 7/2/07

"Amnesty means that you've got to pay a price for having been here illegally, and this bill does that."

George W. Bush, on an immigration reform bill, Washington, D.C., 6/26/07

"The Constitution gives the President the power of clemency to be used when he deems it to be warranted. It is my judgment that a commutation of the prison term in Mr. Libby's case is an appropriate exercise of this power."

George W. Bush, statement released
by the White House, 7/2/07

WHY DICK CHENEY IS SO SECRETIVE ABOUT WHAT GOES ON IN HIS OFFICE

In late June, a House committee released documents showing that for the past four years, Cheney's office had fought to be exempted from regulations covering the handling of classified material, claiming that they were not fully part of the executive branch. In a blistering eight-page letter to Cheney, Rep. Henry Waxman (D-Calif.) said, "Your office may have the worst record in the executive branch for safeguarding classified information."

"He's not part of the executive branch. We're not going to fund something that doesn't exist ... I'm following through on the vice president's logic, no matter how ludicrous it might be."

Rep. Rahm Emanuel (D-III.) explaining his threat to cut off $4.8 million in executive-branch funding for the vice president's office, Washington, D.C., 6/26/07

"[Bush administration officials] believe that they should be able to do what they want to do, and that the law is a minor obstacle."

Bill Clinton,
Des Moines, Iowa, 7/5/07

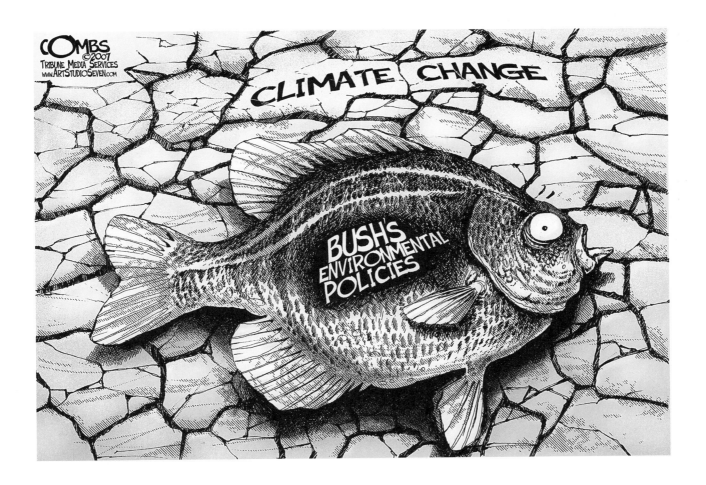

"Wisdom and strength, and my family, is what I'd like you to pray for."

George W. Bush, Washington, D.C., 5/2/07

Build the Presidential Library on the Moon

On July 2, 2007, George W. Bush made it clear why he should never be "misunderestimated," despite the public's persistent tendency to do just that. With his approval ratings plunging into the swamp of presidential iniquity, facing what looked to be another round of bipartisan pushback against his "surge" strategy in Iraq, watching his Grand Old Party splinter into squabbling special interest groups, and having just seen the immigration bill—his last great stab at leaving behind a domestic policy legacy—get Tasered into submission, Bush did something that made sense to few people but himself. Bush, who had until then issued fewer pardons and commutations than any commander-in-chief in more than a century, announced the commutation of Lewis "Scooter" Libby's thirty-month prison sentence (for perjury and obstruction of justice during the investigation of the outing of former CIA agent Valerie Plame).

By commuting Scooter's sentence, Bush blithely ignited another firestorm of criticism, apparently oblivious to the conflagration already blazing around him. Only days later, Sen. Pete Domenici (R-N.M.) became the third Republican senator in two weeks to call for a reduction of American forces in Iraq. At the same time, Richard "Big Dick" Cheney continued his Orwellian crusade to redefine reality on his own terms, using the executive power of his office to argue that the vice president wasn't part of the executive branch and so didn't have to abide by its rules. You could almost hear the cartoonists' knuckles cracking as they prepared to whip up this latest crop of tasty morsels into an all-you-can-eat buffet.

And yet, the Pardon that Dare not Speak its Name, as much as it invited controversy at a time when most lame-duck presidents would have been hungry for whatever approval they could get, was par for the course. Bush is not, after all, a president who ever worried about how he was thought of by the public. As recently as May 30, 2007—when the public's approval for the war was lurking below 40 percent—Bush spoke about modeling an extended military presence in Iraq on South Korea, where thousands of U.S. troops have been garrisoned for over half a century.

Given the president's state of supernatural disconnect—think *The Man Who Mistook His Nation for a 10-Gallon Hat*—one wonders how Bush believes he will be remembered by future generations. If events up till now are any indication, and this book is ample evidence that not much has changed over Bush's two terms, one could be forgiven for thinking it might unfold something like this: Sometime in the not-too-distant future, an announcement will be made that, instead of building the George W. Bush Presidential Library at Southern Methodist University in Texas (currently planned to house a 40,000-square foot public policy institute and 145,000-square foot library),

construction will shift to a roomy locale somewhere in the Sea of Tranquility.

Or to a long-dry canal on Mars.

If that happens, Bush is certain never to be misunderestimated again. Of course, as Harry Bliss points out (below), the instant Bush leaves office he will be sorely missed by comedians and cartoonists all over planet Earth.

BIOGRAPHIES

The Cartoonists
HARRY BLISS

Bliss is a renowned cartoonist, children's book illustrator, and *New Yorker* magazine contributor. His daily cartoon panel, 'Bliss,' is syndicated by Tribune Media Services and runs in newspapers across the country. He has drawn 17 covers and numerous cartoons for the *New Yorker*. The long list of children's books he has illustrated includes *A Fine, Fine School, Diary of a Worm*, and *Mrs. Watson Wants Your Teeth*. Bliss has received awards of excellence from *Print* magazine, *Communication Arts* magazine, *Inc.* magazine, the Society of Illustrators, the National Society of News Design, and the Art Directors Club of New York. Bliss has studied at The Pennsylvania Academy of the Fine Arts, The University of the Arts, and Syracuse University. He lives in Burlington, Vt., with his son Alex.

PAUL COMBS

Combs is the most recent addition to the family of cartoonists syndicated by Tribune Media Service, joining TMS in 2006. After working as an editorial cartoonist for the *Tampa Tribune*, Combs decided to seek a less hectic lifestyle for his family. He returned to his native Ohio, where his unique work is published in the *Defiance Crescent-News*. He also works as a firefighter/instructor for the Bryan (Ohio) Fire Department.

PAUL CONRAD

Conrad, a three-time winner of the Pulitzer Prize (1964, 1971, 1984), was chief editorial cartoonist of the *Los Angeles Times* from 1964 to 1993. He has also won two Overseas Press Club awards, and in 1997 the Society of Professional Journalists honored him with his seventh Distinguished Service Award for Editorial Cartooning, making him the only journalist to win that many SPJ awards in any category since the annual competition began in 1932. Conrad also had the distinction of appearing on Richard Nixon's "Enemies List" in the early 1970s. Conrad and his wife, Kay, live in Palos Verdes, Calif., and have four children.

MATT DAVIES

Davies has been the editorial cartoonist for *The Journal News* (New York) since 1993. He received the Pulitzer Prize in 2004 and has won many other awards, including the inaugural Herblock Prize in 2004 and a 2001 Robert F. Kennedy Award for a collection of work highlighting subjects such as police brutality, racism, and school overcrowding. Born in London, Davies moved to America as a teen and studied at the Savannah College of Art and Design in Georgia and at the School of Visual Arts in New York. He is a past president of the Association of American Editorial Cartoonists. Davies lives in Connecticut with his wife and two daughters.

WALT HANDELSMAN

Handelsman won the 2007 Pulitzer Prize for editorial cartooning and won his first Pulitzer in 1997. His long list of honors also includes the 1989 and 1993 National Headliner Award, the 1992 Society of Professional Journalists Award, the 1996 Robert F. Kennedy Journalism Award, and the 2003 Scripps Howard National Journalism award. Handelsman has been the editorial cartoonist for *Newsday* (New York) since 2001 and has also worked for the *New Orleans Times-Picayune*, the *Scranton Times*, and a chain of suburban weeklies in Baltimore. A graduate of the University of Cincinnati, Handelsman has published eight collections of his editorial cartoons and a children's book. He lives in Woodbury, N.Y., with his wife and two sons.

DAVID HORSEY

Horsey, the *Seattle Post-Intelligencer*'s editorial cartoonist since 1979, won the Pulitzer Prize for editorial cartooning in 1999 and 2003 and was a finalist in 1987. He also received the National Press Foundation's 1998 Berryman Award for cartoonist of the year, and the Society of Professional Journalists has given him 14 first-place regional awards. He is a graduate of the University of Washington and holds a master's degree from the University of Kent at Canterbury in England. Horsey has published five collections of cartoons, and he served as president of the Association of American Editorial Cartoonists in 2000–01. He and his wife live in Seattle and have two children.

TAYLOR JONES

Jones' syndicated caricatures have run in newspapers both in America and abroad, appearing in publications such as *Ma'ariv* (Israel), *Courrier Internationale* (France), and *El Mercurio* (Chile). He wrote and illustrated *Add-Verse to Presidents*, a satirical look at the presidency from George Washington to Ronald Reagan, and he has illustrated a series of books on the language of sports, including *How to Talk Baseball* and *How to Talk Golf*. Jones is a native of Long Island, N.Y., and a graduate of a small college in Iowa. He and his family currently reside on Staten Island, N.Y.

DICK LOCHER

Locher has been an editorial cartoonist for the *Chicago Tribune* since 1973 and was awarded a Pulitzer Prize in 1983. That was also the year in which Locher began illustrating the long-running comic strip *Dick Tracy*, which he continues to draw to this day. He has authored or co-authored numerous *Dick Tracy* books and collections of his editorial cartoons. Locher has won the prestigious John Fischetti Editorial Cartoon Award and dozens of other awards. Born in Dubuque, Iowa, Locher studied art at the Chicago Academy of Fine Arts and the Art Center of Los Angeles, and he has served in the U.S. Air Force. Locher and his wife reside in suburban Chicago and have two children.

CHAN LOWE

Lowe has been the editorial cartoonist for the *South Florida Sun-Sentinel* since 1984 and was a Pulitzer

Prize finalist in 1990. He has won many awards for his work, including the Berryman Award from the National Press Foundation in 2000 and the 1992 Green Eyeshade Award. A kinetic sculpture by Lowe was exhibited in 1997 at the National Gallery for Caricature and Cartoon Art in Washington, D.C. Lowe graduated from Williams College in Williamstown, Mass., and lives in Palm Beach County, Fla.

DOUG MARLETTE

Marlette (1949–2007) was most recently the editorial cartoonist for the *Tulsa World*, having also worked at the *Tallahassee Democrat*, *Newsday* (New York), the *Atlanta Journal-Constitution*, and the *Charlotte Observer*. He won the Pulitzer Prize in 1988 and received three National Headliners Awards. In addition to the 19 books of cartoons to his name, Marlette was also a prolific writer who penned two novels and numerous magazine articles. Marlette's first novel, *The Bridge*, was voted Best Book of the Year for Fiction by the Southeast Booksellers Association in 2002 and was purchased by Paramount Pictures. Marlette graduated from Florida State University.

JACK OHMAN

Ohman signed a syndication agreement with Tribune Media Services while he was still a college student at the University of Minnesota, becoming the youngest cartoonist to ever be nationally syndicated, at age 19. He is now the editorial cartoonist for *The Oregonian* in Portland, where he has worked since 1983, and has also worked for the *Columbus Dispatch* and the *Detroit Free Press*. Ohman has produced eight books, and in 2002 he received the National Headliners Award. He also won the Overseas Press Club Award in 1995. He lives in Portland with his three children.

DREW SHENEMAN

Sheneman has been the editorial cartoonist for *The Star-Ledger* (Newark, N.J.) since 1998, when he joined the newspaper two weeks after graduating from Central Michigan University and became the youngest full-time editorial cartoonist in the country at the age of 23. He has won the John Locher award, handed out by the Association of American Editorial Cartoonists, and the Charles Schulz Award. Sheneman lives in Bedminster, N.J., with his wife and daughter.

WAYNE STAYSKAL

Stayskal worked for the *Tampa Tribune* from 1984 to 2003, and he has also cartooned for the *Chicago Tribune* and the *Chicago American*. He has produced several books, including *It Said Another Bad Word*, *Liberals for Lunch* (with syndicated columnist Cal Thomas), and *Till Euthanasia Do You Part*. Stayskal graduated from the Chicago Academy of Fine Art in 1956 and got his professional start in commercial art. He and his wife live in St. Charles, Ill.

DANA SUMMERS

In addition to drawing editorial cartoons for the *Orlando Sentinel*, where he has worked since 1982,

Summers also draws the nationally syndicated comic panel *Bound and Gagged* and teams with fellow *Sentinel* cartoonist Ralph Dunagin to produce the popular comic strip *The Middletons*. A graduate of the Art Institute of Boston, Summers has won awards from the Overseas Press Club and the Society of Professional Journalists. He was born in Lawrence, Mass., and lives in Orlando with his wife and three children.

DAN WASSERMAN

Wasserman joined the *Boston Globe* in 1985 and is a member of the *Globe*'s editorial board. Wasserman's cartoons have appeared in publications such as *Time*, *Newsweek*, and *The Economist*, and he has authored two books: *We've Been Framed* and *Paper Cuts*. A graduate of Swarthmore College in Pennsylvania, Wasserman is a native of New Haven, Conn., who now resides in the Boston area with his wife, two kids and three cats.

DON WRIGHT

Wright, the editorial cartoonist for the *Palm Beach Post* since 1989, won the Pulitzer Prize in 1966 and 1980 while working for the *Miami News*. He has twice won the Sigma Delta Chi Award for Distinguished Service in Journalism and has won numerous other awards. Wright has authored several collections of comics, and in addition to his work as a political cartoonist, he has been an award-winning newspaper photographer and graphics editor. Born in Los Angeles, Wright lives in Florida.

The Writers
PATRICK FITZMAURICE

Fitzmaurice has been an editor with Tribune Media Services since 2000 and has worked with dozens of nationally syndicated writers and cartoonists. He was also an editor at *Pro Football Weekly* and Thomson Target Media in Chicago, and at CNI Newspapers in Milwaukee. Fitzmaurice is a Milwaukee native and a graduate of the University of Wisconsin-Madison. He lives in suburban Chicago with his wife and two children.

GARRISON KEILLOR

Keillor is the author of more than a dozen books, including *Lake Wobegon Days*, *The Book of Guys*, *Love Me*, and *Homegrown Democrat*. He is also the creator, host, and writer of the shows *A Prairie Home Companion* and *The Writer's Almanac*, both heard on public radio stations across the country. He won a Grammy Award in 1987 for Best Spoken Word Album for the audiobook: *Lake Wobegon Days*. In 2006, Robert Altman's film, *A Prairie Home Companion*—which Mr. Keillor wrote and also co-starred in—was released, and he also opened an independent book-store in St. Paul called Common Good Books. His columns appear weekly on *Salon.com* and are distributed by Tribune Media Services to newspapers across the country. September 11, 2007 saw the publication of his new novel, *Pontoon*, by Penguin Books. Mr. Keillor is a member of the American Academy of Arts & Letters. He was born in Anoka, Minn. in 1942 and graduated from the University of Minnesota. He lives in St. Paul with his wife and daughter, and also has a son and two grandsons.

MARK CRISPIN MILLER

Miller is a professor of Media, Culture and Communication at New York University, and a media critic with an international reputation. His books include *Boxed In: The Culture of TV, The Bush Dyslexicon, Cruel and Unusual: Bush/Cheney's New World Order,* and *Fooled Again: The* Real *Case for Electoral Reform,* which recently came out in paperback with over 100 pages of new material. In the summer of 2004, he wrote and performed in *A Patriot Act* at the New York Theater Workshop. (The show was also made into a movie by that title, now available on DVD.) Miller also is the General Editor of "American Icons," a book series published by Yale University Press, which will be bringing out his study of the Marlboro Man in the fall of 2008. *News from Underground,* Miller's blog on politics and media, is on-line at www.markcrispinmiller.com. He lives in Manhattan with his wife and son and their unusual black cat.

CARTOON INDEX